I0465247

From
Freshman
to
Fortune 500

7 Secrets to Success
for Grads, Undergrads, and Career Changers

Marky Stein

Fortune 100 Consultant
Best-Selling Author of *Fearless Interviewing*
Contributor to the *Wall Street Journal*

FROM FRESHMAN TO FORTUNE 500
SEVEN SECRETS TO SUCCESS FOR GRADS, UNDERGRADS, AND CAREER CHANGERS

Copyright © 2016 Marky Stein.

All rights reserved. No part of this book may be used or reproduced by any means, graphic, electronic, or mechanical, including photocopying, recording, taping or by any information storage retrieval system without the written permission of the author except in the case of brief quotations embodied in critical articles and reviews.

iUniverse books may be ordered through booksellers or by contacting:

iUniverse
1663 Liberty Drive
Bloomington, IN 47403
www.iuniverse.com
1-800-Authors (1-800-288-4677)

Because of the dynamic nature of the Internet, any web addresses or links contained in this book may have changed since publication and may no longer be valid. The views expressed in this work are solely those of the author and do not necessarily reflect the views of the publisher, and the publisher hereby disclaims any responsibility for them.

Any people depicted in stock imagery provided by Thinkstock are models, and such images are being used for illustrative purposes only. Certain stock imagery © Thinkstock.

ISBN: 978-1-5320-0795-8 (sc)
ISBN: 978-1-5320-0796-5 (e)

Library of Congress Control Number: 2016918613

Print information available on the last page.

iUniverse rev. date: 03/15/2017

To my mother, Rusty Stein,

who taught me by example and through her
ministry everything that is truly important in life

Praise for Marky Stein's Best-Selling Fearless Series

Fearless Interviewing: How to Win the Job by Communicating with Confidence (McGraw-Hill 2003)

- #1 interviewing book of the "100 Best Career Books of All Time"—onlinecollege.org
- #2 of the "100 Inspirational Books Every Job Seeker Should Read"—onlineuniversities.com

"Marky Stein's book is wonderful. She gives us a thorough analysis of the whole interviewing process. *Fearless Interviewing* is clear, kind, and full of good advice ... highly recommended."

> —Barbara Sher, Best-selling author, *Live the Life That You Love*, www.barbarasher.com

"If your library can contain only one book on interviewing, then *Fearless Interviewing* is it."

> —Richard Knowdell, Executive Director, Career Planning and Adult Development Network, President, Career Research and Testing

Fearless Career Change: The Fast Track to Success in a New Field (McGraw-Hill 2005)

"Kudos to Marky Stein for writing such a practical, inspired, and wise book."

> —Barbara Sher, Best-selling author, *Refuse to Choose*

"Marky's unique way of eliminating fear of failure and fear of success makes it easy to make a career change at any age. Her techniques are light years ahead of the competition."

> —Paul Roberts, Host and Producer, 1550 Today, WNTN 1550 Radio, Newton-Boston

"Marky Stein's *Fearless Career Change* is the perfect guidebook for those people who want to transition to a more meaningful career without having to start from scratch."

> —Margot King, Host of nationally syndicated radio show *Job Talk*

*Fearless Resumes: The Proven Method to Get
a Great Job Fast* (McGraw-Hill 2009)

"Marky cuts to the core of what it takes to quickly attract the eye of an interviewer. She skillfully guides readers through an ingenious step-by-step process leading to a powerful and uniquely customized resume. Marky Stein's book is sure to be a winner for the serious job seeker."

—Lynn Joseph, PhD, author of *The Job Loss Recovery Program
Guide: The Ultimate Visualization System for Landing a Great
Job Now*, www.DrLynnJoseph.com

"Marky Stein's book is all about sales. How to hit the employers' 'hot buttons' and get their attention right off the bat, how to keep them 'hooked' all through the résumé, and how to dramatically increase the probability of 'closing' with an invitation to an interview. She's definitely got the strategy job seekers need to win the important meetings and coveted job offers they desire."

—Mitch Gooze, author of *Value Acceleration: The Secrets to
Building an Unbeatable Competitive Advantage*

*From Freshman to Fortune 500
7 Secrets to Success for Grads, Undergrads, and Career Changers*

"In FROM FRESHMAN TO FORTUNE 500, Marky Stein has hit a home run! The 7 job-search strategies she lays out in the book are fast, effective, and extremely cost-effective. PLUS, they really work! In each short chapter, Ms. Stein succinctly describes how effective these tactics can be with compelling case studies from actual clients and personal anecdotes. This book is filled with great advice, and in it, Marky shares insights that have long been hidden from the general public and student populations. Kudos!"

—Erica Golden, Career Coach and author of *"RESUMES THAT
HACK THE JOB HUNT: Write Resumes that Get Results...
Right Now!"* www.ericagolden.com

Filled with scores of practical guidance, tools and resources for job-seeking students and grads. Marky's seven strategies are practical and current with inspiring examples from her own private practice. I will definitely be recommending it to my students!

—Dr. Lynn Joseph, LA Metro Faculty Chair, DeVry University.
Best-selling author, *The Job Loss Recovery Program Guide.*
www.joblossrecovery.com

Contents

Acknowledgments ix

Introduction: How the Seven Secrets Will Help You Find Your
Dream Job... xi

Chapter 1: Secret #1: Grab the Skills Employers Want in
Less Than Six Weeks for Less Than $200 1

Chapter 2: Secret #2: Skyrocket Your Marketability with
Free Accredited Certifications 32

Chapter 3: Secret #3: Design a Career Change or Earn a
Raise with Strategic Education.. 40

Chapter 4: Secret #4: Beat the Competition to a Fortune
500 Internship 47

Chapter 5: Secret #5: Catapult Yourself into a New Field
by Volunteering 54

Chapter 6: Secret #6: Ascend the Ladder from an Entry-
Level Position to an Executive Position............................. 59

Chapter 7: Secret #7: Gain Work Experience in a Part-Time,
Flexible Job with Benefits 64

Conclusion: Your Magnificent Brain.. 67

Index... 75

About the Author... 79

Acknowledgments

I would like to acknowledge the following people who knowingly or unknowingly have affected my life, my thoughts, my career, and my spiritual growth (in no particular order): Jill Stein, Melissa Greer, Marty Bonsall, Darlene Korb, Robin Ogden, Pat Cross, Erica Golden, Lisa Gonzales, Maria Euen, Krishna Roman, Robin Belkin, Richard Bolles, Astrid Berg, Angeles Arrien, Emmett Miller, Barbara Sher, Kate Smith, Linda Higgins, Michael, Adam, Amy Frost, Lynn Joseph, Bob Proctor, Anthony Robbins, Brian Tracy, Georgia Galassi, Patria Jacobs, Nina Goldin, Vicki Trent, Adrian Zubrin, Jack Canfield, Midge Robinson, Meg Harlor, Eckhart Tolle, and, most of all, H. P.

Introduction

How the Seven Secrets Will Help
You Find Your Dream Job

*G*etting *from college to the real world can be scary*. And waiting to
get a four or six-year degree before you can work in the field of your
dreams can be frustrating. So can graduating from a bachelor's, master's,
or even doctoral program and finding that you don't have the practical
experience or real-world marketable skills to find a job.

It's discouraging to not be able to find a job that relates to your
interests and your college degree. And having to go back to school to get
an advanced degree when you want to change careers is expensive and
time consuming. This book is here to help you with that!

I'd like to tell you a bit about my background helping students and
adults in a wide variety of settings, careers, and industries.

I am a three-time best-selling author of job-seeking and career-
transition books, a career coach, a Fortune 100 consultant, and a
contributor to the *Wall Street Journal*. I formed my own career-coaching
company in 1992, serving **students and executives in just about every
industry and college major**. I am the author of three McGraw-Hill career
classics: *Fearless Interviewing: How to Win the Job by Communicating
with Confidence, Fearless Career Change: The Fast Track to Success in
a New Field*, and *Fearless Resumes: The Proven Method for Getting a
Great Job Fast*. I was also the career question-and-answer columnist,
"The Interview Expert," on the popular job-seeking site, Monster.com
for ten years.

My first book, *Fearless Interviewing*, has been named the number one interviewing book of the *"100 Best Career Books of All Time"* by onlinecollege.org as well as number two of the *"100 Inspirational Books Every Job Seeker Should Read"* by onlineuniversities.com.

In 2015, I had the honor of being recognized by LinkedIn as *"one of the nation's top career experts"* and in 2017 I was asked to be on the Advisory Board of College Recruiter, *www.collegerecruiter.com*, rated by Forbes as one of the leading job search websites in the world.

From 1998 to 2006, I worked as a Career Consultant for more than seventy-five Fortune 500 companies, including Capital One Financial, Levi-Strauss, IBM, Hewlett-Packard, Sun Microsystems, Becton-Dickenson, Toshiba, Dell, Fujitsu, and many others.

I bring twenty-five years of experience in helping people start careers, chart short- and long-term career goals, change careers, learn new skills, upgrade skills, get raises, and get jobs.

The seven secrets I'll be sharing in this book can be combined to *help you break into even the most difficult occupations and industries*, start working in the field you love while you earn your degree, and change careers by spending as little money and time as possible.

The secrets I'm sharing in this book can be implemented in a rather short time frame—*sometimes in as little as a few weeks and most in considerably less than six months.* I'm certainly not saying that you can substitute these short-term secrets for a college education.

Getting as high a degree as possible will make a huge difference in your lifetime earnings!

- Statistics from many studies, particularly one conducted by the US Department of Education's National Center for Education Statistics (NCES), state that a typical worker with a Bachelor's degree earns, on average, about $20,000 more per year than a person with a high school education. A Master's degree earns more than $25,000 on average per year than a Bachelor's degree, and getting a PhD can put you into the category of earning, on average, at least $100,000 more per year!

- Those with bachelor's degrees earn about 64 percent more over a lifetime than those with only a high school diploma.

- The unemployment rate is also higher among those who do not possess a college degree.

So *the seven secrets in this book are meant to augment your college education, not replace it.*

Degrees We'll Be Talking About

- anthropology
- art
- biochemistry
- biology
- business administration
- chemistry
- classic literature
- computer information systems
- computer sciences
- creative writing
- educational counseling (career counseling)
- electrical engineering
- environmental studies
- film
- hospitality
- human resources
- law
- liberal studies
- logistics
- marine biology
- marketing

- mechanical engineering
- nursing
- pharmacy
- physical therapy
- political science
- psychology
- public administration
- public health
- radio and television broadcasting
- social work
- sociology
- software engineering
- theater arts
- veterinary medicine
- vocational rehabilitation counseling
- zoology

What You'll Learn in This Book

You're going to hear how about how thirty or more students, graduates, and career changers started in their first jobs or internships, earned their careers by taking entry-level jobs directly related to their long-term goals, or changed careers *swiftly and with as little expense as possible*. You'll see how some of them took strategic steps like volunteering or even enrolling in just one class to achieve their goals. You'll learn how they used one or more of the seven secrets in this book to find jobs they love and are passionate about.

You'll be able, by example, to apply these secrets to your own life and boldly step out on the way to a job in the Fortune 500 sector or a smaller company that really uses your talents, education, and personal and professional passions! Does this sound like something you would like to do? I assume that the answer is yes.

I'd like to assist you in finding the position of your choice in Fortune 500, Fortune 1000, and Fortune 100 companies like Apple, Cisco, Price Waterhouse Cooper, AT&T, Pacific Gas and Electric,

Lockheed-Martin, Google, Becton-Dickenson, and Levi-Strauss. I'd also like to help you break into smaller companies in manufacturing, health care, telecommunications, science, information technology, defense, environmental services, nonprofit, education, entertainment, biotech, retail, and pharmaceuticals. You'll also find out how many students and grads found jobs in medical, finance, and law offices.

What's the fastest and least expensive route to your dream job? This book is about how you can take the fastest and least expensive route to working directly in the industry of your choosing now—or at least in the next six to twelve weeks—without having to spend a lot of money to get there!

- Terry got to work right away in a physical therapy clinic as an Aide while he was studying for his Master's degree in Physical Therapy.

- Shaniqua volunteered for six weeks at a vocational rehabilitation company and got hired as a Vocational Rehabilitation Counselor as soon as a new position opened up.

- Marie used just one class as "strategic education" to make a career change from being a Landscaper to an Ecologist and tripled her salary.

- Mohammed found a great job as a Paralegal by taking a twelve-week accredited (and free) certificate program while he went to law school.

- Fatima leveraged her Fortune 500 internship into a job as a Software Engineer while she studied for her Master's degree.

- Li got started as a Lab Technician while she was earning her Bachelor's degree in Chemistry.

- Martin started as an entry-level television Production Assistant and worked his way up to Executive in Charge of Production by learning on the job.

I'm going to release every secret I have used to help these students, grads, and career changers succeed, and I can guarantee that I have some secrets you have never heard from a friend, parent, teacher, or career-counseling professional. In fact, to the best of my knowledge, almost all of the pointers and secrets in this book have never been printed or published before.

I want to share these secrets with you because you deserve to know them. You have already applied (or soon will devote) a great deal of time, tens of thousands of dollars, and thousands of hours of effort into your college major. You deserve to find work that is compatible with your interests and field of study.

How does that sound? Perhaps this sounds impossible!

Are you doing what you love or settling for less? It could be that you have already settled for a job unrelated to your college major because you couldn't find anything else and just fell into something "convenient" to help you accomplish the very necessary task of supporting yourself or a family. You've told yourself that someday you will get back to your dream, but you have not had the time or energy to do it—yet! Maybe you've thought about spending $20,000 or $60,000 or more on getting a more advanced degree because you think it will make you more marketable, but you can't afford it or you're afraid of a lifetime of student debt. Perhaps you've even completely given up and abandoned your once-cherished career dream for a job unrelated to your life's dream because that seems more secure and pragmatic. After all, doesn't being a Dolphin Trainer sound a little bit silly or crazy? In this book, you'll learn how Tim, a Marine Biology graduate, got an opportunity as a Dolphin Trainer in Hawaii!

I wrote *From Freshman to Fortune 500:*

- to *save you time* by presenting proven shortcuts for getting to work right away in the field you're aiming for;

- to *save you money*—80 percent of the secrets presented in this book cost either nothing or less than $200 to implement; and

- to *prevent* you from having to go through the anxiety, agony, *frustration, and depression* of working in a job you don't really like because it seems impossible to find the job you originally intended to do.

Is Your Work Related to Your College Major?

Do you know that only 7 to 32 percent of people end up finding jobs related to their college major (*Washington Post*, May 20, 2013)? That's a pretty daunting number when you think of the time and money you spent (or are going to spend) on getting your degree.

If you are a student, plan on enrolling in any level of college, or are unable to find a job in your major field of study after graduation, this book is for you! If you'd like to make a career change and want to do it in less than ninety days, you will also find this book useful.

I'm aware that your target job may not be aimed at the Fortune 500 sector and that you may want to aim at a smaller company or even a start-up. The techniques in this book are equally effective for both small and large companies.

Choosing a Career You Love

No matter what you decide to do and what sort of companies you're aiming for, the really important thing is that you love what you do! You're probably going to spend about *one-third* of the total hours of your life at work.

Why not do something you love?

The biggest predictor of success (earnings, productivity, happiness, satisfaction, and meaning) is that you love what you are doing. If you love what you're doing, you may not always know *how* to do everything associated with that job or everything about how to advance in that career, but you'll be *motivated* to learn it.

Let's take a look at the seven secrets that will help you get that dream job!

The Seven Secrets

1. **Grab the Skills Employers Crave in Less Than Six Weeks for Less Than $200**
   We're going to take a look at how several online self-paced classes can make all the difference in breaking into a field you love.

2. **Skyrocket Your Marketability with Free Accredited Certificates**
   Find out how you can get free or partially government-subsidized training at the American Job Center closest to your home.

3. **Earn a New Job or a Raise with Strategic Education**
   Just one college-level class can change your branding (the employer's perception of you), help you with your career change, and/or get you a promotion or a substantial raise in pay.

4. **Beat the Competition to a Fortune 500 Internship**
   Learn how to use a secret, free database to locate a person inside a company through the "hidden job market" to dramatically increase your odds of winning a strategic internship.

5. **Catapult Yourself into a New Field by Volunteering**
   Do you know that as little as six days to three months of volunteering at the right kind of organization can build up your résumé and get you hired?

6. **Move from Entry-Level to Executive Positions**
   Read real stories of people who learned on the job and went from $30,000 a year to more than $180,000 a year—and how you can too.

7. **Gain Work Experience in a Part-Time, Flexible Job with Benefits**
   Build your résumé, get valuable recommendations, and enjoy health, dental, retirement, vision, vacation, and other benefits while you work at a part-time job that gives you time for your studies.

Work in the Field You Love Right Away

What's your long-term goal? Wouldn't it be great if you could start doing it—or something closely related to it—right away? If you're already doing something related to your college major, wouldn't it be fantastic to explore a short-term, no- or low-cost method for upgrading your skills and getting a higher salary?

I've assisted students and clients just like you who were scared, frustrated, confused, or even completely lost get back on track and into jobs they now cherish. It's my hope to be able to do the same with you!

Let's get started!

Chapter 1

Secret #1: Grab the Skills Employers Want in Less Than Six Weeks for Less Than $200

Have you ever wished that you didn't have to wait four or eight years or more to start working in the field of your passion? Well, now you don't have to wait that long. Let me tell you about Terry, Sharon, and others who were able to break into their fields by using the strategy of grabbing the skills employers crave in only six weeks!

Salary Information

I'll also be including some salary information from the US Department of Labor's website (www.onetonline.org) to give you an idea of the salary range of certain job titles throughout this book.

Since the city of Los Angeles is about in the middle range of the cost of living in the United States as a whole, I'm going to use it as an index to calculate the low and high ends of an annual salary expectation for the job titles mentioned in this text. Please keep in mind that in other parts of the country the salary could be higher than in Los Angeles—even as much as $50,000 a year higher. Also, in some parts of the country, the lower end of the range might be even lower than in Los Angeles.

If you want to know the range of salary (either hourly or annually) for just about any of seventy thousand job titles in your own local area, you can do this by going to the O*NET (www.onetonline.org) and researching the high and low salary ranges for just about any job title in your state or local area.

By the way, you can research just about any job title and find out loads of information about the duties, educational requirements, job market demands, typical work environment, related job titles, and salary information on the O*NET.

Don't underestimate the value of a recent Certificate in a given occupation. The O*NET does not list any certificates under its education section. It only lists Associate, Bachelor's, Master's, and high school diplomas. Your *recent up-to-date* Certificate may be just as valuable as an older Bachelor's or Associate degree!

Finding a Position in Your Field While Earning Your Degree

Name: Terry
Education: Freshman, BS, Biology
Short-term goal: Physical Therapist Aide ($21,040 to $38,450)
Long-term goal: Physical Therapist ($61,640 to $117,110)

Terry was nineteen years old when he began his freshman year at a university. While playing high school football, he had sustained an injury to his shoulder. He had to go to a Physical Therapist at a sports medicine clinic to get it worked on. He was fascinated by the rehabilitation process and established a great rapport and respect for his therapist.

He already knew before entering his freshman year that he wanted to be a Physical Therapist. He also knew from the academic counselor at his college that it would require at least six years of math, sciences, anatomy, physiology, kinesiology, and biochemistry before he could attain his Master's degree and become licensed as a Physical Therapist.

Although he was extremely motivated to study and gain the education that he needed for licensure, he told me that he wished it just wouldn't take so long before he could start working in a physical therapy clinic.

I suggested a short and affordable way that he could get right into a physical therapy clinic as a Physical Therapist Aide while he was earning his BS in Biology and then studying in a Master's program in Physical

Therapy in order to become a licensed. His solution was a ***six-week online course called Ed2Go (www.ed2go.com), and it cost him only $199!*** He eagerly completed the online course in less than six weeks and earned a Certificate as a Physical Therapist Aide.

Here is a copy of his résumé after he completed his training:

Terry Nguyen
San Francisco, CA
232-555-7777
terry_nguyen@tmail.net

Objective

A position as a Physical Therapist Aide

Summary

Recent Certificate as a Physical Therapist Aide specializing in strength, balance, and coordination exercises. Over one year as a customer service representative. Won employee-of-the-month award in January 2016 at Home Depot. Experienced in serving more than one hundred customers per day and dealing well with difficult customers. Currently enrolled in a course of study leading to a Bachelor of Science degree in Biology with the plan to attain a Master's degree in Physical Therapy. Patient, motivating, follows directions.

Relevant Classes

Human Anatomy	Rehabilitative Exercises	Hot and Cold Therapy	Balance Exercises
Human Physiology	Patient Charting	Strength Exercises	Coordination Exercises

Employment History

Customer Service Representative / Cashier, Home Depot, San Francisco, CA 2015–present

- Operate cash register and accept credit cards, debit cards, checks, and cash for more than one hundred customers daily
- Verify appropriate customer identification for accepting checks
- Direct customers to find products they are looking for throughout the store
- Stock shelves with equipment and products on an as-needed basis
- Give advice to customers regarding purchases in the garden department on an as-needed basis
- Deal diplomatically and politely with difficult customers

Education

Currently enrolled in a course of study leading to a BS in Biology, San Francisco State University, San Francisco, CA
High school diploma with a 3.8 GPA, Sunset High School, San Francisco, CA

Volunteer Experience

Volunteer Sports Coach, Middleton Elementary School, After-school program, San Francisco, CA

Cold Calls Really Work

Once we pulled his résumé together, I urged him not to wait for a job opening to appear on the Internet. I suggested that he telephone every physical therapy clinic in the area. He called about twelve physical therapy clinics, including those at hospitals, stroke-rehabilitation centers, chronic pain management, and sports medicine facilities.

Finally, one of the clinics offered him twenty-five hours per week as a part-time permanent employee with full medical, dental, vision, 401(k), and a retirement plan. His schedule was flexible so he was able to arrange his work around his classes. He took the offer and worked there while he was going to school.

Terry was delighted to work at a physical therapy clinic where he could observe and learn his new field and perform basic physical therapy techniques. He led and supervised patients in therapeutic exercises, applied hot and cold packs, and completed other duties. He also learned the daily operations of the clinic and was able to watch Physical Therapists performing advanced procedures on patients.

His responsibilities increased with time, and he was able to put his experience on his résumé. And he loves his job!

What if you're not like Terry—and you're not sure about the type of job you might be interested in? It's perfectly natural to feel that way, whether you're twenty or sixty years old!

From Copywriter to Technical Writer

Name: Peter
Education: BA, Creative Writing
Present job: Copywriter (this particular job paid him $15 per hour)
Target job: Technical Writer ($48,180 to $111,960)

Peter graduated with a Bachelor's degree in Creative Writing from a liberal arts university. Just after graduating, he got a Copywriter job writing classified ads for a local newspaper. He came to see me as a career-coaching client because he was dissatisfied with the position and wanted a higher salary. He told me that he felt lost in his career and was beginning to suspect that a job in writing was not for him. Peter didn't want to be an English teacher, a Professor, a Poet, or a Prose writer, and he really didn't know what to do with his degree.

I knew there were several other options that could be available to him with his expert knowledge of the English language and excellent written communication skills. Among many other careers, he could be a Grant

Writer for a corporation or a nonprofit organization, a Marketing and Communications professional for a corporation, a Publicist, a Journalist, a Technical Writer, an Editor, Proofreader or other options. I gave Peter a *career-interest assessment* to determine how his natural interests could best be used in a career setting. He took the O*NET Interest Profiler on the ***www.onetonline.com*** website (under a purple box on the website that says "My Next Move"). His interests suggested a possible career in Technical Writing or Desktop Publishing. He researched the two careers on the O*NET website and learned the typical duties of the jobs, the knowledge and education needed, the demand for the position in the job market, and the salaries of the positions and more. (It is very important, if you decide to take this assessment, that you understand the career titles are only suggestions for further research. Your results on the assessment do not indicate that you "should" do a certain career. Visiting the career counselor at your school or alumni career center, discussing your options, and taking other career assessments are good ideas.)

After performing his Internet research, Peter decided to enroll in a Technical Writing Certificate program through Ed2go. Soon after graduation, he found a new position with a considerably higher salary than his advertising job. He learned from his local salary research on the O*NET that after seven to eight years on the job, he could easily command a salary of $145,000 a year or more.

From Veterinary Assistant to Veterinarian

Name: Jessica
Education: Pursuing a BS in Zoology
Short-term goal: Veterinary Assistant ($19,210 to $43,330)
Long-term goal: Veterinarian ($64,430 to $187,200 or more)

Jessica loved animals. At home, she had two dogs and one cat. While she was getting her undergraduate units in zoology, hoping to enter veterinary medicine, she worked as a cashier at a pet store. Like Terry (the Physical Therapist Aide), she didn't want to have to wait six years to get her advanced degree before she could begin handling animals. She wanted to get even closer to animals, but she didn't know how to do it. I suggested that she take three certificate classes from Ed2Go to prepare her to become a Veterinary Assistant. This job would permit her to work directly in the treatment center of a Vet's clinic and be able to handle animals. She easily passed her classes and was delighted to find a job that focused strictly on animal care and gave her valuable experience toward her goal of becoming a Veterinarian while she was completing her studies.

From Registered Nurse to Home-Based Business in Medical Billing and Coding

Name: Max
Education: Registered Nurse (MS, Nursing)
Present job: Registered Nurse ($65,070 to $125,060)
Target job: Home-Based Business in Medical Billing and Coding ($26,150 to $72,780)

Max and Cindy took family planning seriously. They decided, after two years of marriage, to try for two children. Both of them considered their careers to be serious lifelong pursuits. Max was a Registered Nurse in a large hospital. Cindy was an Electrical Engineer for an electronics firm. They decided that, for their first child, Cindy would stay home and Max would work. Once their first child was in preschool, Max would stay home with their new infant. He wanted to continue in the healthcare field and start a home-based business in Medical Billing and Coding. He took an Ed2Go class and mastered the codes of diseases and their treatments. He was able to work part-time at home while Cindy worked as a way to make sure he had plenty of time with the kids. To start his business, he took some free business, accounting, and marketing classes from the United States Small Business Administration (www.sba.gov) at his local chapter of the organization. He also received free advice on how to run a service business from home with no-cost mentorship services from SCORE (www.score.org).

From Grant Writer to Social Worker

Name: Sharon
Education: BA, Anthropology; earning an MS in Social Work
Short-term goal: Grant Writer ($48,180 to $111,960)
Long-term goal: Social Worker ($37,300 to $92,160 or more)

Sharon had a Bachelor's degree in Anthropology and was earning a Master's degree in Social Work. She hoped to be able to work on behalf of senior citizens in a nonprofit agency.

While she was working on her degree, she wanted to start working for a senior citizens' agency. I recommended that she take two courses from Ed2Go.com where she could gain the skills to work at a nonprofit and get her foot in the door. She took a six-week Gerontology (the study of aging) class online as well as an online and Grant-Writing course and earned certificates in both. Each class cost $199.

We went to a database called data.com (www.data.com) and looked up real names and contact information of real people (in this case, the Volunteer Coordinator or Executive Director) in the nonprofit industry at agencies serving senior citizens in her area.

She found a name at the Council on Aging and contacted the Volunteer Coordinator. They were writing a grant regarding low-cost housing for senior citizens and needed volunteers to do research on the grant. She was able to use her new knowledge of grant writing to volunteer. The grant was successful, and she gained valuable experience to add to her résumé. On top of getting a taste of working in a senior services organization, she received a stellar letter of recommendation from the Executive Director.

Her two certificates, volunteer experience, and letter of recommendation will serve her well when she is ready to work full-time as Social Worker for senior citizens.

The Ed2Go catalog is massive and full of some really valuable six-week online classes. For less than $200, you can break into a new field, augment your degree, launch a career, or upgrade your skills for a higher salary.

From Writing Tutor to Editor

Name: Ingrid
Education: PhD, Classic Literature
Present job: Self-employed Writing and Reading Tutor (she charged $30 an hour)
Target job: Editor ($33,060 to $123,210)

Ingrid loved to tutor children and adults in reading and writing, but she was tired of the financial ups and downs of running her own business. She wanted to work with colleagues and not be alone running her own business. She wanted a solid job surrounded by other co-workers with whom she could interact that offered her benefits and room to grow. I gave her an online personality preference assessment called the *Jung Typology Test* that is similar to the widely used Myers-Briggs Type Indicator. She took the assessment free at *www.humanmetrics.com* and then looked up her results at *www.truity.com*.

Of the sixteen possible personality types, she received ENFJ - Extraverted, Intuitive, Feeling, Judging. We will not discuss all of the implications, *of which there are many*, with this result. If you want to learn more about the Jung Typology test, take the assessment on your own and study the results and their meanings on www.truity.com. A book that will give you tremendous insight on your personality preference and its implications on what types of job titles may be appealing to you is *"Do What You Are"* by Tieger and Barron-Tieger.

When Ingrid looked into her results she found that one of the jobs she may enjoy would be an Editor. (*As with any assessment, you may want to discuss your results with a career-counseling professional*). She easily passed the Ed2Go six-week class and set her sights on working for a major publishing house as a fiction editor. As it turns out, her first job was with a weekly local newspaper as a Copyeditor. Within a year, she found her dream job as an Editor at a large publishing house with full health, dental, vacation, holiday, 401(k), and retirement benefits.

From Event Planner to Marketing Director

Name: Freda
Education: Sophomore, BS, Marketing
Short-term goal: Event Planner ($28,140 to 92,880)
Long-term goal: Marketing and Communications Manager ($69,610 to $187,200 or more)

Freda found the world of public relations, communications, and marketing vital and exciting. Her goal was to get a job in the marketing department of a Fortune 1000 high-tech company. She also loved volunteering to plan events, such as weddings for friends and relatives and activities for her sorority. With a certificate in events planning (called "Wow, What an Event!" in Ed2Go) and her volunteer experience, she was able to get a job as a marketing intern in the marketing department assisting with Event Planning at a Fortune 500 telecommunications company.

There are many entry-level jobs to be found in the field you're targeting while you're getting the advanced credentials from your college to achieve your long-term goals. Use your imagination (and think about consulting with a career counselor at your college or alumni career center) as you scan through the list below and think of some of the jobs you could get with the following low-cost, six-week online certificates.

The Ed2Go Course Catalog

Below is an example of some of the Ed2Go catalog. Unlike some online classes, Ed2Go allows you to ask questions and interact with your instructor via e-mail! It even has classes on how to open and market your own business!

Accounting

Accounting Fundamentals

Gain a marketable new skill by learning the basics of double-entry bookkeeping, financial reporting, and more.

Accounting Fundamentals II

This course will build on the knowledge you gained in the Accounting Fundamentals course to provide you with a solid understanding of corporate accounting practices.

Introduction to QuickBooks 2014

Gain control of your business as you learn to use this powerful accounting software to create and print invoices, track your payables and receivables, and more.

Intermediate QuickBooks 2014

Master the advanced features of QuickBooks and learn to manage multiple company files, create customer statements, enter price levels for inventory, and much more.

Performing Payroll in QuickBooks 2014

Learn how to use QuickBooks 2014 to create paychecks, pay taxes, generate forms, and produce dazzling reports.

QuickBooks for Contractors 2014

Learn how to use the Premier Contractor Edition of QuickBooks 2014 for your construction business to create contract estimates, perform time tracking and job costing, generate powerful reports, and much more.

Business and Administration

Achieving Success with Difficult People

Learning how to have more successful relationships with difficult bosses, coworkers, students, neighbors, or relatives.

Administrative Assistant Applications

Gain the skills and knowledge you'll need to prepare for the Certified Administrative Professional exam and begin a rewarding career as an administrative assistant.

Administrative Assistant Fundamentals

Prepare to take advantage of the many new job opportunities in health care, legal services, and other industries.

Building Teams That Work

What are the secrets to managing successful teams in the workplace? Explore communication techniques and problem-solving skills that will help you get your team on track in no time.

Business Finance for Non-Finance Personnel

This course will help you understand business environments, financial statements, and strategy so you can make more profitable business and personal financial decisions.

Distribution and Logistics Management

Learn how to improve your company's distribution and logistics management activities, increase customer satisfaction, and improve operational throughput.

Fundamentals of Supervision and Management

Learn the people skills required to motivate and delegate, and learn tools for solving problems and resolving conflicts.

Fundamentals of Supervision and Management II

Learn how to be an effective manager or supervisor. Master the basics of communicating effectively, and learn tools for developing your own interpersonal skills.

High-Speed Project Management

Learn to deal with the realities of managing projects at supersonic speeds despite truncated timelines, inadequate staffing, and skimpy budgets.

Interpersonal Communication

Become aware of the conscious and unconscious codes of meaning we send when communicating with others.

Keys to Effective Communication

Lost for words? Don't be! Learn to build rapport, trust, warmth, and respect through conversation.

Keys to Effective Editing

From the language of editing to grammar, punctuation, and syntax to the all-important relationships between editor, author, and publisher, every facet of editing will be explored in this copyediting course.

Intro to Business Analysis

Learn powerful techniques to improve decision-making skills at work organization by understanding how to identify and meet customer needs.

Manufacturing Applications

Increase efficiencies and productivity by learning to apply the principles and concepts of manufacturing.

Manufacturing Fundamentals

Learn the basic skills required to work in the manufacturing field.

Mastery of Business Fundamentals

Acquire practical experience in strategic planning, management, and finance without enrolling in an MBA program.

Mastering Public Speaking

Learn the secrets of effective public speaking and small-group communication.

Project Management Applications

Experienced project manager teaches you tricks of the project-management trade.

Project Management Fundamentals

Gain the skills you'll need to succeed in the fast-growing field of project management.

Purchasing Fundamentals

Improve your company's bottom line by mastering the fundamentals of purchasing.

Six Sigma

Total Quality Applications: Learn to apply the elements and methods of Six Sigma to achieve the highest possible quality.

Skills for Making Great Decisions

Learn how to make excellent everyday decisions from an experienced counselor and life coach. You'll master techniques for achieving your goals, managing risk, dealing with crisis, and making decisions—big and small—with knowledge and confidence.

Supply Chain Management Fundamentals

Master the fundamentals of supply chain management and prepare for internationally recognized certification examinations.

Total Quality Fundamentals

Learn the basics of total quality management.

Understanding the Human Resources Function

Learn to handle basic human resource functions to ensure the best possible results.

Internet Security Certification Prep

Basic CompTIA A+ Certification Prep

Start preparing for CompTIA A+ certification as you learn PC basics and troubleshoot in a real-world PC environment.

Intermediate CompTIA A+ Certification Prep

Take the second step toward becoming a CompTIA A+ certified tech by mastering virtualization, printers, and three flavors of the Windows operating system.

Advanced CompTIA A+ Certification Prep

Finish your CompTIA A+ Certification Prep by learning how to select, install, and service video, sound, and portable computers, and how to network, secure, and troubleshoot.

CompTIA Security+ Certification Prep 1

Master the terms and concepts you need to pass the CompTIA Security+ exam and earn your Security+ certificate.

CompTIA Security+ Certification Prep 2

Continue to prepare for the CompTIA Security+ exam as you review the information you need to pass the test and earn this important certification.

Advanced PC Security

Use ethical hacking techniques to locate and close security holes in your own network.

CompTIA Network+ Certification Prep

Prepare to take and pass the CompTIA Network+ exam and begin a career as a network tech.

Project Management

PMP Certification Prep 1

Begin a well-paying career as a project manager by preparing to take and pass the PMP certification exam.

PMP Certification Prep 2

Prepare to take and pass the Project Management Institute's PMP certification exam.

Computer Fundamentals

Understanding the Cloud

Learn everything you need to truly understand the cloud, including how it works, what drives it, why it's so popular, and how to make the cloud work for you.

Computer Skills for the Workplace

Gain working knowledge of the computer skills you'll need to succeed in today's job market.

Introduction to Windows 7

Get up to speed quickly on Microsoft Windows 7 with this fun and easy hands-on course for beginners.

Keyboarding

Learn how to touch-type or improve your existing typing skills using Keyboarding Pro 5.

What's New in Microsoft Office 2013?

Get up to speed on the exciting new features of Microsoft Office 2013, including Word, Excel, PowerPoint, Access, Outlook, OneNote, and Publisher.

Introduction to Microsoft Excel 2013

Become proficient in using Microsoft Excel 2013 and discover countless shortcuts, tricks, and features for creating and formatting worksheets quickly and efficiently.

Intermediate Microsoft Excel 2013

Take your Microsoft Excel 2013 skills to the next level as you master charts, graphs, PivotTables, Slicers, Sparklines, AutoFilter, macros, and other advanced Excel functions.

Advanced Microsoft Excel 2013

Master advanced features and functions of Microsoft Excel 2013, including analysis tools, data tables, PivotTables, and conditional formatting.

Introduction to Microsoft Word 2010

Learn how to create and modify documents using Microsoft Word 2010, the world's most popular word processing program.

Intermediate Microsoft Word 2010

Master the more advanced features of Microsoft Word 2010 and learn how to create an index, build a list of figures, design a table of contents, do desktop publishing, perform a mail merge, and use time-saving shortcuts.

Introduction to Microsoft PowerPoint 2013

Learn how to use Microsoft PowerPoint 2013 to create animated presentations formatted with color, text, pictures, shapes, charts, and text and object hyperlinks.

Database Management and Programming

Introduction to Database Development

An experienced professional guides you through a structured approach to database design and development.

Introduction to Microsoft Access 2013

Learn to build, edit, and maintain a database in Access 2013, using tables, reports, forms, and queries to give you fast access to all your important information.

Intermediate Microsoft Access 2013

Expand your Microsoft Access skills to build better, more user-friendly Access databases.

Introduction to Oracle

Learn how to use the Oracle database-management system to plan, organize, and manage your data.

Intermediate Oracle

Learn how to write powerful and flexible PL/SQL programs.

Introduction to SQL

Gain a solid working knowledge of the most powerful and widely used database programming language.

Intermediate SQL

Expand your knowledge of Structured Query Language (SQL), the industry-standard database programming language.

Introduction to Visual Basic

Learn how to write code for Windows applications using the Visual Basic programming language and development environment.

Grant Writing and Nonprofit Management

A to Z Grant Writing

Learn how to research and develop relationships with potential funding sources, organize grant-writing campaigns, and prepare proposals.

Advanced Grant Proposal Writing

Learn how to develop successful, fundable grants from experts in the field. Gain a full understanding of the criteria funders use to determine whether your grant proposal gets funded or rejected.

Writing Effective Grant Proposals

Learn to prepare grant proposals that get solid results for your favorite organization or charity.

Introduction to Nonprofit Management

Develop the skills and secrets you need to become an integral part of one of America's fastest-growing service sectors.

Marketing Your Nonprofit

Further the ideals and goals of your nonprofit by learning to compete more effectively for members, media attention, donors, clients, and volunteers.

Nonprofit Fundraising Essentials

Learn the basics of fundraising for nonprofit organizations, from annual and special fund drives to more advanced projects involving corporate and foundation relations, major gifts, and planned giving.

Starting a Nonprofit

Industry veteran shows you how to take a nonprofit business from vision to reality.

Health Care

Explore a Career as a Pharmacy Technician

Master the skills that will prepare you for an entry-level position as a pharmacy tech or clerk, and discover the steps you can take to become a Certified Pharmacy Technician (CPhT).

Become a Physical Therapy Aide

Prepare for a rewarding career as a valued member of the physical therapy team.

Become an Optical Assistant

Learn what it takes to become an optical assistant, and discover why it's one of today's most popular and fascinating career opportunities.

Become a Veterinary Assistant

A practicing veterinarian prepares you to work in a veterinary office or hospital.

Become a Veterinary Assistant II: Canine Reproduction

Practicing veterinarian teaches you to manage the entire canine breeding cycle, from assessing the health of parents to puppy care.

Become a Veterinary Assistant III: Practical Skills

Learn the practical skills you'll need to be a valuable veterinary assistant or educated pet owner.

Certificate in Food, Nutrition, and Health (16 Contact Hours)

In this certificate program, you'll gain a holistic overview of current food and nutrition issues and their impact on physical, social, emotional, and spiritual health.

Certificate in Gerontology (44 Contact Hours)

Earn a certificate proving you have the skills required to meet the health-care needs of a rapidly aging population.

Explore a Career as an Administrative Medical Assistant

Learn all about the in-demand career of medical information management as you explore the job of an administrative medical assistant (AMA) in a doctor's office from appointment scheduling and chart creation to medical billing and coding.

Explore a Career in Medical Coding

Learn how to use the CPT manual and the ICD-9-CM to find medical codes for any disease, condition, treatment, or surgical procedure.

Explore a Career in Medical Transcription

Learn how to transcribe the medical reports most often used in health care today, and discover how to get started and advance as a medical transcriptionist.

Law

Explore a Career as a Paralegal

Find out if a paralegal career is the perfect choice for you, as you explore the fundamentals of United States law and legal terminology.

Employment Law Fundamentals

Learn the basics of employment law so you can legally hire, evaluate, and manage employees.

Workers' Compensation

Gain essential skills and a solid understanding of one of the fastest-growing areas in law.

Criminal Law

An in-depth look at criminal law and the real world of prosecutors, defense attorneys, and the paralegals who work closely with them.

PC Networking and Security

Introduction to PC Security

Security expert teaches the fundamentals of PC and network security.

Advanced PC Security

Use ethical hacking techniques to locate and close security holes in your own network.

Introduction to Networking

Learn the fundamentals of networking and prepare for a career in a new and fast-growing field.

Intermediate Networking

Gain practical experience in a hot new career field. Topics include VPNs, security, and Internet connectivity.

Introduction to PC Troubleshooting

Learn to decipher and solve almost any problem with your PC.

Wireless Networking

Industry expert shows you how wireless networking works, as well as how to plan, deploy, and connect to wireless networks.

Sales and Marketing

Business and Marketing Writing

Write great marketing copy to improve your company's image and your chances of getting hired or promoted.

Marketing Your Business on the Internet

Develop an Internet marketing plan for your business that incorporates SEO, advertising, e-mail, social media, and more.

Small Business Marketing on a Shoestring

Discover small business marketing secrets that can help you attract attention, woo your target audience, grow your customer base, and expand your profits for little or no money.

Professional Sales Skills

Discover how to begin a successful and rewarding career in sales.

Start Your Own Business

Creating a Successful Business Plan

Turn your business ideas into a solid plan for financing and long-term success.

Wow, What a Great Event! Event Planning

Looking for a fun new career coordinating special events? Learn proven techniques from a master event planner.

Start Your Own Small Business

Stop dreaming and learn how to start your own successful small business.

Start and Operate Your Own Home-Based Business

An experienced entrepreneur teaches you how to develop the motivation, discipline, and creativity to quit your job and be your own boss.

Web and Computer Programming

Creating Mobile Apps with HTML5

Learn to use HTML5, CSS3, JavaScript, jQuery, and web APIs to create cross-platform mobile apps and mashups.

Introduction to Programming

Take your first steps toward a career as a computer programmer as you master basic programming concepts and get hands-on practice in writing applications containing GUIs, sound, and graphics.

Introduction to Ajax Programming

Learn Ajax programming and discover how to use the technologies that comprise Ajax (HTML, JavaScript, XML, PHP, and more) to create web applications with desktop-like performance.

Introduction to C# Programming

Learn the fundamentals of computer programming with the new C# programming language.

Intermediate C# Programming

Learn to write Graphical User Interface programs in the C# programming language.

Introduction to C++ Programming

Learn to program in C++, even if you have no prior programming experience!

Introduction to Java Programming

An experienced Java programmer introduces important Java topics with clear, step-by-step instructions.

Intermediate Java Programming

Deepen your understanding of the Java programming language, and start writing programs that are more sophisticated and professional.

Intermediate PHP and MySQL

Learn how to create a dynamic, interactive online store using advanced PHP techniques and a MySQL database server.

Introduction to PHP and MySQL

Learn how to create dynamic, interactive websites using PHP and a MySQL database server.

Introduction to Python 2.5 Programming

Learn the fundamentals of computer programming in Python with topics that include basic decisions and loops, advanced data structures, object-oriented programming, and graphical user interfaces.

Introduction to Python 3 Programming

Enhance your knowledge by adding Python to your programming skills.

Mac, iPhone, and iPad Programming

Learn to create Mac, iPhone, and iPad apps and programs using Objective-C and the Xcode compiler.

Graphics and Web Page Design

Creating Web Pages

Learn the basics of HTML so you can design, create, and post your very own site on the web.

Advanced Web Pages

Take your web-development skills to the next level as you learn how to create advanced websites using CSS, HTML5, media queries for mobile devices, interactive forms, and embedded video.

Introduction to ASP.NET

Learn how to create powerful, interactive, community-based websites with ASP.NET.

Introduction to CSS3 and HTML5

Learn to create state-of-the-art websites using modern CSS3 and HTML5 techniques.

Intermediate CSS3 and HTML5

Take your CSS3 and HTML5 skills to the next level and learn how to create professional-quality websites.

Advanced CSS3 and HTML5

Learn how to use exciting new features in CSS3 and HTML5 to design animated interactive websites for desktops, laptops, and mobile devices.

Introduction to Dreamweaver CS6

Learn to create web pages, layouts, and websites using CSS formatting options and other tools with Adobe's industry-standard web-design application.

Creating WordPress Websites

Learn how to use WordPress, a free and popular web-design tool, to quickly and easily create attractive blogs and interactive websites.

Intermediate WordPress Websites

Discover how to create and maintain dynamic websites and blogs without technical coding using the self-hosted WordPress.org publishing platform.

Writing and Editing

Fundamentals of Technical Writing

Learn the skills you need to succeed in the well-paying field of technical writing.

Effective Business Writing

Improve your career prospects by learning how to develop powerful written documents that draw readers in and keep them motivated to continue to the end.

Writing Essentials

Master the essentials of writing so you can excel at business communications, express yourself clearly online, and take your creative literary talents to a new level.

The Keys to Effective Editing

If you aspire to be an editor, this course will teach you the fundamentals of top-notch editing for both fiction and nonfiction.

A six-week $199 investment, combined with your college degree, could turn into a well-paying new job! There is so much that the Internet has to offer today to people beginning, improving upon, and changing careers, and this trend will continue to grow and flourish into the future.

Other Online Programs

Some other free and very low-cost options for taking programs (some from top universities like Harvard, Yale, and MIT) online are:

- **www.mooc.com**
- **www.coursera.com**
- **www.gcflearnfree.org**
- **www.universalclass.com**
- **www.edx.org**
- **www.lynda.com**
- **www.udemy.com**
- **www.study.com**
- **www.alison.com**

Another great resource is Universal Class (*www.universalclass.com*). Universal Class presents short-term accredited classes that also offer college Continuing Education Units (CEUs)

From Clinical Psychology to Wellness Coaching

Name: Madelyn
Education: PhD, Clinical Psychology
Short-term goal: Wellness Coach Certificate
Long-term goal: Wellness Coach (she charged from $85 to $125 per hour)

Madelyn had just graduated from a Clinical Psychology PhD program. She came in to career coaching with me because she was confused about her career direction. She really thought she might have wasted her years in school because, in the last year of her training, she realized that she didn't want to work with people with mental illnesses.

She was much more interested in human potential and optimum physical and mental well-being than she was in helping patients with mental health issues. After a period of some coaching and career exploration, she decided that she wanted to use her skills and knowledge about psychology and counseling to become a Wellness Coach. Wellness coaching is a very fast-growing field, and many major hospitals now employ coaches to assist patients with stress reduction, nutrition, exercise, disease prevention, and lifestyle choices.

Essentially, Madelyn had almost all of the skills, but she needed to "rebrand" herself in the employer's eyes from being a doctor of clinical psychology to being a wellness coach. I suggested that she use inexpensive, short, college-accredited courses from Universal Class.

I suggested that she complete three online self-paced Certificate classes from the site, for which she would also gain CEUs (Continuing Education Units from the International Association for Continuing Education and Training). The Certificate courses I suggested were as follows:

- Wellness Coaching
- Nutrition
- Life Coaching

Because Universal Class has a payment option that includes an unlimited number of classes in one month for fifty-nine dollars, her whole "rebranding" process cost almost nothing! We wrote her a new résumé that reflected her new Certificates, and she found a job at a major hospital as a Wellness Coach. She's elated about helping people to reach their full healthy potential and well-being!

Finding the Missing Piece for a Career in Marketing

Name: Rosa
Education: AA, Marketing
Short-term goal: Marketing Specialist ($35,520 to $121,280)
Long-term goal: Marketing Manager ($69,610 to $187,200 or more)

Rosa graduated with an AA in Marketing and was eager to get a job in her field while she studied to earn her MBA (Master's in Business Administration).

She had just started her Bachelor's degree in Marketing and wanted a part-time position so she could complete her studies as soon as possible. The trouble was that every job opening she found required the use of a customer-relationship management (CRM) database called Salesforce.

Normally, Salesforce classes were expensive but she was able to find a Salesforce training class for only forty dollars on the website Udemy (*www.udemy.com*). This one special skill made her much more marketable. She soon had multiple offers and opted for an entry-level job at a Fortune 1000 company.

You might consider free or low-cost online courses to catapult you into your next new entry-level, midlevel, or advanced-level career move! What do you think?

Next we're going to talk about slightly longer free or federally subsidized accredited programs through a government agency that is *right at your doorstep*!

Chapter 2

Secret #2: Skyrocket Your Marketability with Free Accredited Certifications

D o you know that five to forty-five minutes away from your home, there may very well be a place where you can get up to $10,000 worth of occupational training for free (that you never have to pay back!) or with a partial subsidy from the government?

Yes, you can!

American Job Centers

In the United States, there are thousands of government-sponsored Career Centers that offer a variety of three- to six-month nationally accredited programs. Many programs are offered in conjunction with colleges and universities or short-term vocational training. They don't offer degrees but they do have vocational, professional and accredited Certificate programs.

These government career centers are known as American Job Centers and are still sometimes referred to as One-Stop Career Centers. You can easily locate the nearest Center near you by going to *www.servicelocator.org* and entering your local zip code.

These facilities can be used by *anyone* with a legal right to work in the United States. They serve unemployed, underemployed (working part-time but desiring full-time work or working for a lower wage than wanted), retired and even employed people. *They also serve students*. Their face-to-face classroom occupational and professional trainings are usually conducted at night and/or on weekends, so you can attend them even if you're currently in school or working. Some offer Internet-based Certificates so that you can access them in a self-paced online program from home or anywhere there is a computer with an Internet connection.

- Would you like to start working in an entry-level job in the field of your interest (short-term goal) while you pursue an advanced degree (long-term goal)?

- If you're already working and have a degree, would you like to upgrade your skills with a recent and relevant certificate so that you can change careers or command a higher salary?

- If you've just earned your Associate, Bachelor's, Master's, or higher degree but find that your studies at school equipped you with chiefly theoretical but very little practical knowledge that would equip you to fit the job descriptions out there in the marketplace, would you like to take a look at some free programs that will increase your marketability?

- If you had to take a job completely unrelated to your degree (which can happen up to 70 percent of the time, according to the *Washington Post* study in the last chapter) just to keep financially afloat, would you like to get back to what is really your passion by getting a nationally recognized accredited Certificate that will put you back in touch with your original career dreams?

- Would you like to change careers and get the government to pay for your training?

If you answered "yes" to one or more of these questions, enrolling today at a One-Stop Career Center may be a viable solution for you!

For example, you might have a long-term goal of becoming a Physician, Pharmacist, Lawyer, Architect, Art Director, Information

Technology Director, or Materials/Supply Chain Manager which require a considerable amount of time and education.

With the types of certificate programs offered by Career Centers, you could break into your field of interest as a:

- Pharmacy Technician
- Paralegal
- CAD Architectural, Civil or Mechanical Drafter
- Graphic Artist
- Medical Assistant
- Logistics Technician
- Computer Network Administrator
  or other short-term careers while you're studying for your advanced degree.

Here are a few short examples of students who opted to work in the fields of their long-term goals by earning ***nationally recognized and free certificates***.

Name: James
Major: Biochemistry
Short-term goal: Pharmacy Technician ($23,650 to $64,830)
Long-term goal: Pharmacist ($77,100 to $171,830)

Name: Mohammed
Major: Political Science
Short-term goal: Paralegal ($36,870 to $103,670)
Long-term goal: Lawyer ($72,300 to $187,200)

Name: Cynthia
Major: Art
Short-term goal: Graphic Artist ($30,470 to $96,270)
Long-term goal: Art Director ($48,810 to $187,200 or more)

Name: Li
Major: Chemistry
Short-term goal: Lab Technician ($22,920 to $75,960)
Long-term goal: Chemist ($42,830 to $131,910)

Name: Natasha
Major: Logistics
Short-term goal: Logistics Technician ($50,540 to $121,820)
Long-term goal: Supply Chain Manager ($67,420 to $187,200 or more)

The following are some examples of people who got certified at a One-Stop Career Center and were able to command higher salaries.

From Software Engineer to Salesforce Developer

Name: Minh
Education: MS, Software Engineering
Present job: Software Engineer ($64,660 to $150,320)
Target job: Salesforce Developer (she was making about $90 an hour)

Minh had a Master's degree in Software Engineering with two years of experience as a Software Developer and was making about seventy-two dollars an hour. She wanted to specialize in something that would bring her larger financial returns right away. She took a free accredited three-month Salesforce Developer Certificate class and immediately got employed in a long-term contract in a Fortune 500 Company that now pays her ninety dollars an hour.

From Customer Service Manager to Project Manager

Name: Abdul
Education: BA, Business Administration
Present job: Customer Service Project Manager (he was making about $85,000)
Target job: Telecommunications Project Manager ($38,020 to $122,030)

Abdul had a Bachelor's in Business Administration and some experience out of the country as a Customer Service Project Manager in the Information Technology (IT) industry. He completed a Certificate program in Professional Project Management (PMP) at a One-Stop Career Center that was associated with a major university that met nights and weekends for eight weeks. He then received career advising, help with updating his résumé, and interview coaching at the Center. The PMP program was offered *at no cost* to him. In addition to this, he completed an elite course in Agile/Scrum methodologies for Project Managers and a course in advanced Microsoft Project (both also free). He passed the project management (PMI) test and found his first job in the United States as a Telecommunications Project Manager starting at $100,000 a year with full benefits and perks!

From Customer Tech Support to Software Engineer

Name: Melinda
Education: AS, Computer Information Systems
Present job: Computer-User Support Technician ($33,140 to $81,830)
Target job: Software Engineer ($64,660 to $150,320)

With a recent AS in Computer Information Systems, Melinda was aiming to hit the job market and start her search. Even though she felt confident about her training, she asked if I thought there were any more skills or software languages that would make it easier for her to break into the field as a Software Engineer. Yes! There is an increasingly popular language called *Python* that makes it easier to break into the field and offers a substantial pay increase for an entry-level position. A person with an AS in computer sciences would typically start at a salary of about $79,050 per year. However, the same person who has knowledge of Python programming—just one course—would start at about $90,400 per year. Python training was being offered free at her local Career Center. With just three months of studying the popular skill, her potential starting salary was increased by more than $10,000 per year!

From Adjunct Professor to Marketing Demographics Specialist with Transferable Skills

Name: Zahada
Education: PhD, Sociology
Present job: Adjunct Professor (she was making less than $50,000 a year in this part-time position)
Target job: Marketing Research Analyst ($35,520 to $121,280)

Zahada came to my office and declared that she was a "burned-out" and "underpaid" PhD. She had been working as an Adjunct Professor of Sociology at a community college and came to the conclusion that she would never find full-time work or tenure. We first talked about her "transferable" skills.

Transferable Skills

Transferable skills are skills you have learned in *one occupation* or industry that could be "transferred" or used in **another occupation or industry**. For example, if you have the skills to be a customer service representative in the retail industry, it is likely that you could use your "people" and "problem-solving" skills to get a job at a nonprofit, in the finance, hi tech or another industry.

If you were a Project Manager in the pharmaceutical industry, you could use your leadership, logistics and budgeting skills to be a Project Manager in the medical devices, telecommunications, manufacturing or other industries.

In this regard, Zahada had gained the skills of using quantitative and qualitative research and data analysis in demographics (the study of certain segments of the human population) while earning her degree and writing a dissertation for her Doctorate in Sociology. We reasoned that she might be able to use those skills in the field of Marketing Intelligence as a Marketing Research Analyst.

In the field of marketing, it is highly valued to be able to recognize patterns in certain segments of the population (demographics) for many reasons, including age, geographic area, education, values, and buying habits. All Zahada had to do was transfer her skills in demographics and "rebrand" herself as a marketing professional. In other words, she had to get the hiring managers in the marketing profession to *perceive* her as a marketing professional. She took a short-term accredited course from her local One-Stop Career Center in marketing and put it on her résumé as a recent Certificate. She was able to break into a Fortune 500 company as a Marketing Research Analyst in a full-time position with benefits that were over $30,000 more than her previous earnings.

Other Examples of Accredited Certificates

There are many more incredible opportunities like these available to you at your local career center. Some examples of accredited programs (approximately three months in duration) from a government career center in California are as follows:

- Accountant
- Administrative Assistant
- Agile/Scrum Project Management
- AutoCAD drafting (architectural, civil, 3D and mechanical drafting)
- Business Analyst
- CCNA (Cisco-Certified Network Administrator)
- Child Development
- Cosmetologist
- CompTIA Certificate
- Culinary Arts
- Cybersecurity
- EKG Technician
- Electrician
- Electronics Technician
- Environmental Resource Management
- Financial Analyst
- Green Technology (Alternative Energy)

- Human Resources Generalist
- Information Technology Project Manager
- Marketing and Communications
- Massage Therapist and Health Educator
- Laser Technologist
- Advanced Manufacturer
- CNC Machinist
- Medical Assistant
- Phlebotomist
- Psychiatric Technician
- Six Sigma Black Belt (quality assurance)
- Web Developer
- Oracle Financials
- Graphic Artist
- Database Developer
- Microsoft Office Specialist
- Bookkeeper
- Pharmacy Technician
- IC Layout Designer
- Software Programming and others

Programs at Your Local Career Center

This is not a complete list of accredited programs. Your own One-Stop Career Center may only have some of these programs or more of them. I hope this list gets your mind buzzing with possibilities for your own career growth!

I want you to join me in taking a look at some other incredible success stories of people using a technique called "strategic education," a very short-term solution to breaking into the career of their choice!

Meanwhile, be sure to find your local career center at *www. servicelocator.org* and explore their offerings. One of them might be just right for you!

Chapter 3

Secret #3: Design a Career Change or Earn a Raise with Strategic Education

All advertising, sales, and marketing people are familiar with the term *branding*. Branding is different from marketing and sales because marketing, effectively, says, "Buy me." Branding sends a subtly different message. Branding says, "This is me ... are you interested?" You can **brand and rebrand** yourself in your résumé and interview.

Branding and Employer Perceptions

Branding yourself in a particular way for a particular job or industry means that you are creating an image or **perception** of yourself in the employer's mind. Up to now, you might have considered the concept of branding to be only related to what you have done in the past with your career or education. However, branding can also include *something you are about to do*. We shape an employer's perception of us when we outline *where we are headed* as well as *where we have been*.

Strategic Education

You can do this by using a strategy called *strategic education*. It means **enrolling** in a course of study (**even one class**) that could lead to a college or university degree or professional Certificate.

For example, here is how it might look on your résumé:

- "Currently enrolled in a course of study leading to a Bachelor's degree in Marketing and Communications"

- "Currently enrolled in a course of study leading to a Master's degree in Chemistry"

- "Currently enrolled in a course of study leading to a Master's degree in Electrical Engineering"

These phrases can be similarly used for an Associate, Bachelor's, Master's, or Doctorate degree as long as you are *actually enrolled* in an institution of higher learning. It's very unwise to lie on your résumé or in an interview, but I know that you wouldn't do that!

Strategic education denotes only that you are *enrolled*—not that you have completed study (or even declared your major) in a given department or pursuit.

Of course, if a degree or license is legally required to practice a profession such as a Physician, Attorney, Psychotherapist, CPA or other professions, strategic education will not substitute for a degree or licensure.

I've helped hundreds of students and professionals gain jobs in their chosen occupations by using strategic education.

From Landscaper to Ecologist

Name: Marie
Present job: Landscaper ($19,100 to $46,080)
Target job: Ecologist (Conservation Scientist) ($54,320 to $127,380)

Marie was a landscaper with a BS in Biology from a prominent university. She came to me as a private career-counseling client when she was applying to jobs in Environmental Services. She had a number of reasons she wanted to stop being a landscaper and start working in Environmental

41

Services. For one, she was nearing forty and felt that her body, especially her wrists and back, would no longer hold up in such a physical job.

Although Marie had graduated from a top school, she was having no luck in getting interviews from sending out multiple resumes for Environmental Services or "Ecology" jobs. She suspected that it was because she needed a Master's degree.

I suggested that she enroll in one "Open University" graduate course at a State University to see if we could "rebrand" her. Many colleges and universities allow members of the public to enroll in one or two Open University options for which no formal application, declaration of a major, essays, letters of recommendation, or any of the usual paperwork and procedures for getting admitted to the college are required. Many of these classes are online, but some of them are face-to-face classes.

In this case, all Marie needed to enroll in a Master's level class in the Environmental Studies Department was her driver's license and a credit card. This particular university had a policy that up to a maximum of nine units (about three semester classes) could be taken through this open-enrollment plan without official admission to the degree program. When and if Marie wanted to pursue a master's degree, she could formally apply to the university and use these units earned through Open University toward the degree. She enrolled immediately at the beginning of the next semester (paying about $650 for her one class at that time).

She was admitted a few weeks before the class was to begin. Although her résumé had been rejected by more than twenty Environmental Services organizations, we decided to resubmit it with some new information:

"Currently enrolled in a course of study leading to a Master's degree in Environmental Studies."

Within a few weeks, she was invited to three interviews!

As it turns out, Marie had a stroke of good fortune in the first week of attending class. Her professor asked for any students interested in volunteering on an environmental cleanup project near the San Francisco Bay Area. She volunteered and worked diligently on the project.

Within a few days, an official from a state of California government agency that was cooperating with the university on the project noticed her persistent, hardworking, and professional manner. They gave her a job offer on the spot! This time, it was not volunteering! In fact, it paid three times the amount she earned from landscaping! Now she is tracking the life cycle of baby owls, in order to preserve their species so she still gets to work outside but without the strain to her back and wrists. We'll talk more about how volunteering can help you get noticed in chapter 5.

From Technical Recruiter to Career Counselor

Name: Yuki
Education: BA, Psychology
Present job: Recruiter ($35,260 to $101,740)
Target job: Career Counselor ($34,350 to $99,100)

Yuki had a BA in Psychology and had worked for three years in the Human Resources department of a high tech company. She wanted to find a job where she could use her transferable skills (résumé editing, job interviewing) to directly help people. She decided to become a Career Counselor and centered her job search on government career centers. She wasn't having any luck with those jobs because most of these workplaces required a master's degree in psychology, counseling, education, or human resources. We found an Open University class for her in Educational Counseling at a local university, and she enrolled right away in one class without having to submit transcripts, essays, recommendations, or the normal documentation needed for official admission to the university. When she entered the class, we wrote on her résumé:

"Currently enrolled in a course of study leading to a Master's degree in Educational Counseling."

In her subsequent applications, she received two interviews and was able to land a job in a city Social Services department.

From Public Health Educator to Senior Public Health Administrator

Name: Sam
Education: MA, Public Health (MPH)
Present job: Public Health Educator ($28,700 to $93,980)
Target job: Public Health Administrator (Program Manager) ($43,370 to $125,910)

Sam worked for about seven years for a County Health and Human services department as a Public Health Educator, running programs to educate citizens about AIDS and HIV, smoking, teen pregnancy, and earthquake preparedness. He was ready for a raise in pay and a promotion, but he needed a second Master's degree to get into another salary range as a Public Health Administrator. We enrolled him in an Open University graduate class toward a Master's degree in Public Administration (MPA) that met one night a week. After three semesters—and without finishing the degree—he applied internally for a Program Manager position and was selected out of about forty internal and external applicants. The new position came with a raise of $50,000 per year!

From Attorney to Human Resources Professional

Name: Lupe
Present job: Lawyer ($72,300 to $187,200 or more)
Target job: Human Resources Manager ($54,320 to $127,380)

Lupe was a "burned-out" Employment Attorney. She no longer enjoyed her work as a Lawyer and wanted to move on. She wanted to break into Human Resources in the Fortune 500 sector, but she didn't know how to bridge the gap between her considerable knowledge of employment law and her desire to become a Human Resources Representative. She had to "rebrand" (change the employer's *perception* of her) from an Attorney to Human Resources professional.

Again, using the secret of "strategic education," she enrolled in a university extension program for a Certificate in Human Resources. She added to her résumé:

"Currently enrolled in a course of study leading to a Certificate in Human Resources."

She also took my advice on another wise step toward rebranding herself. She joined a well-known organization for Human Resources professionals called the Society for Human Resources Management.

By joining a ***professional association*** of a profession that you're interested in, you show that you are already "part of the club."

Look up your career—whether it is as a Machinist or an Event Planner—and you are likely to find a professional association that will help your employer *perceive you as already having the intention* to be a practicing professional in your chosen career. Many offer student memberships. You can then say on your résumé:

"Member in good standing in the American Marketing Association" or

"Member of International Association for Electrical Engineers."

By the time Lupe added strategic education and professional-association membership to her résumé, she had no trouble convincing a prominent Fortune 500 information technology company to hire her for a Human Resources position.

From Associate Degree to a Bachelor's Degree

Name: Stuart
Present job: Computer-User Support Specialist ($33,140 to $81,830)
Target job: Software Engineer ($64,660 to $150,020)

Strategic education worked well for Stuart, an experienced Support Specialist and "jack of all trades" with an Associate degree in Liberal Studies. After many years with a small tech company, his whole department was downsized due to the company's financial problems.

He was eager return to work, but he wanted to return to a large, well-known company like Apple, eBay, or Facebook. He wanted to be a

Software Programmer and get a substantial raise in pay. He was a quick learner and passionate about computing.

Although he had learned just about every marketable software language, network protocol, hardware configuration, and computer platform that he needed to succeed at a small company, we found out by reading countless job descriptions for larger companies that a BS in Computer Sciences or a related field would be required in every case.

As soon as he enrolled in one Open University class leading to a Bachelor's degree, we changed his résumé—and he was offered an interview at a Fortune 1000 company. He got the job! Stuart decided to go to classes at night while he works and intends to continue until he earns his Bachelor's degree in Computer Sciences.

You've completed three of the seven secrets, and I hope they're giving you great ideas about how to accelerate your career and improve your life!

Next, we'll explore another short-term plan to break into your first job and/or the job of your dreams!

Chapter 4

Secret #4: Beat the Competition to a Fortune 500 Internship

Have you considered breaking into a world-renowned company or an extremely competitive field? Working as an intern could give you an in. However, internships in the Fortune 500 and Fortune 1000 are extremely competitive. How are you going to beat the competition to one of these coveted opportunities?

Paid or unpaid internships are, without a doubt, one of the best ways to break into many competitive fields. Interns in a variety of industries often get promoted into regular paid positions in the companies for which they are working. They get valuable experience, letters of recommendation, something substantial for their résumés, the ability to define work-related accomplishments at interviews, and contacts with people who can recommend them for paid positions in other companies.

Just about every Fortune 1000 company has an internship program; some of them are paid with wages or a stipend, and some of them are unpaid. Most large companies have more than one office, facility, or plant and may have satellite offices around the United States and abroad. You can find a comprehensive list of Fortune 1000 companies and the addresses of their headquarters at www.geolounge.com.

Some of the companies that have surprisingly high pay for internships are:

- **Google (an average of $6,000 per month)**
- **Proctor and Gamble (average $4,000 per month)**
- **Qualcomm (average $4,800 per month)**
- **Microsoft (average $6,000 per month)**

Companies like Nordstrom, General Electric, and Price Waterhouse Cooper also offer generous compensation for interns, as do many other Fortune 1000 companies. Not all internships are this well paid, but some offer small stipends like $400–$600 per month and priceless training, experience, and opportunities. Highlighting an internship experience on your resume can put you that much closer to your long term goals.

From College to Career at Cisco Systems

One of my career-coaching clients, a technical program manager from Cisco Systems, a Fortune 100 company, spent nine months mentoring twelve new graduates from BSEE (Bachelor's in Electrical Engineering) and MSEE (Master's in Electrical Engineering) programs from around the United States. The new graduates were selected from a group that was recruited by a college recruiter at Cisco. A full 50 percent of them were extended job offers as Network Engineers at Cisco after the mentorship/internship program. That's a great record and a wonderful opportunity, especially since their entry-level salaries started at about fifty dollars and up per hour.

How to Get an Internship

One of the best ways to get an internship (or an entry level position) is to go to the premiere niche job search site, noted by Forbes as one of the top career sites in the world, called *www.collegerecruiter.com*. Another is to go to your college Career Center. Find out if they are sponsoring any job fairs for internships. Get the calendar for job fairs that may be hiring interns in your area and ask a college Career Advisor for help on your résumé, cover letter, and interviewing skills. Also, your Career Advisor may already know of some companies that offer internships for your geographic location and areas of interest and may be able to help you apply for them.

Another way to get an internship is to go to a job search website such as www.indeed.com and simply enter the word "intern" along with the position you're looking for into the search box with the city and state that you're targeting. For example: "Human Resources intern, Houston, TX."

The clear *advantage* of looking for an internship on a job search web site is that you will know that there is a bona fide opening. The difficult-to-overcome *disadvantage* is that you are facing massive competition. There may be a thousand or more looking at the same opening you've found. It's important to be diligent and have a sound strategy for finding and getting an internship because they are comparatively scarce.

Beating the Competition with Direct Contact Techniques

I recommend that you use another strategy, called **direct contact**, which can eliminate your competition by searching for an internship in what is known as the "hidden" or "unadvertised" job market. What is the hidden job market? Very simply, it means that you are searching for a job or internship that exists within a company (or is **planned** to be a future opening) but has **not yet been officially announced or advertised**. Let's take a look at how Fatimah utilized this widely untapped job market.

From Intern to Senior Software Engineer

Name: Fatimah
Education: Junior, BA in Computer Sciences (BSCS)
Short-term goal: Intern (about $4,000 per month)
Long-term goal: Software Engineer ($93,650—$187,200 in the Silicon Valley / San Francisco area)

I started coaching Fatimah when she was in her junior year of earning a Bachelor's degree in Computer Sciences (BSCS). She was looking for a Fortune 1000 internship in Software Programming in the San Francisco / Silicon Valley areas.

I suggested that we directly target College Recruiters and Human Resources personnel who might know about internships in their companies. We found their exact names, titles, street addresses, company phone numbers and websites by using a database called data. com (www.data.com). This is a free database where exact names, titles, and addresses of people in target companies and industries can be found at no cost. With a paid membership (about $250 a year), one can also get e-mail addresses and sometimes direct phone numbers.

In the database, we decided to do an "advanced" search using multiple telephone area codes in her vicinity, looking for the titles "College Recruiter", "Recruiter" and "Human Resources Manager" in Fortune 1000 companies. We found first and last names, job titles, and contact information for more than 100 Human Resources Managers and Recruiters in Silicon Valley.

The names of people Fatimah found were from large and successful companies that are household names like Chevron, Facebook, LinkedIn, Genentech, Google, Maxim, Oracle, The Gap, Pacific Gas and Electric, and more.

Similarly, if you were looking for a College Recruiter in a particular industry (health care, technology, energy, nonprofit, etc.) or in any part of the United States or the world, you could do this at data.com by choosing the title "College Recruiter" or simply "Recruiter". You can search anywhere in the U.S. or the world if you wish. You will find scores of names—with contact information—from a number of companies. I encourage you to try this!

I had Fatimah write letters to the recruiters, indicating a bit about her background and expressing her interest in an internship in a regular "snail-mail" hand-addressed envelope. For those she thought would be particularly good matches, we decided to send via FedEx Ground, because—after all—who can resist opening a FedEx envelope? The same would be true for an envelope sent via UPS or US Priority Mail.

We indicated in the letter, which I call an ***approach letter***, that she would be calling them within seven business days so that her call would be *expected*. She was able to have phone conversations with nine of the recruiters—and two of them had internship opportunities at their companies.

She started as a paid intern at Facebook. Over an eight-year period, while she completed both her BSCS and a Master's degree in Software Engineering, she was hired and promoted to Junior Software Engineer and finally to a Senior Software Engineer, making well over $150,000 a year.

From a Stage Manager to a Film Assistant Director

Name: Kim
Education: AA, Theater Arts
Present job: Stage Manager (salary not listed)
Short-term goal: DGA (Director's Guild of America) Intern (about $3,480 per year plus overtime)
Long-term goal: DGA First Assistant Director ($13,339 to $18,670, DGA Union wage weekly)

Kim enjoyed being a Stage Manager for college and community theater projects, but she only made a stipend of about $500 per production. A production could last up to three months, and the compensation was not enough for her to support herself without help from her parents. She wanted independence and a higher-paying job. She had an interest in the film industry and felt that some of her organizational and logistics experience might pay off if she pursued a goal behind the scenes in the film industry. She stumbled upon a paid internship with the Director's Guild of America. They had internship trainings in Los Angeles and New York. She was one of the very few who was admitted to the program in New York. After the internship, she worked her way up to a union position as a Second Assistant Director to a First Assistant Director and freelanced her way into working on "Movies of the Week" for CBS Television and other networks.

From an AutoCAD Mechanical Drafter to a Mechanical Engineer

Name: Rosa
Education: Pursuing BSME (BS in Mechanical Engineering)

Short-term goal: AutoCAD Mechanical Drafter (she was an intern, but this job would normally pay $35,830 to $79,630)
Long-term goal: Mechanical Engineer ($61,530 to $149,610)

Rosa wanted to start working in the Mechanical Engineering field while she was earning her degree. She went to a One-Stop Career Center and found that they had a three-month free training in one of the essential skills needed for a Mechanical Engineer called AutoCAD Drafting. She found an internship as a mechanical drafter with a Fortune 1000 medical devices company. After she finished her degree, she was hired there as a Mechanical Engineer.

From an Internship at a Community Television Station to a Television Camera Operator

Name: Richard
Education: BA, Radio and Television Broadcasting
Short-term goal: Intern Television Production Assistant (unpaid)
Long-term goal: Television Camera Operator (about $5,500 weekly minimum studio IATSE rate)

Richard, from Atlanta, was an expert in producing, directing, and shooting videos on his own and decided on a career in radio and television broadcasting. He specifically wanted to become a camera operator for a television station. After he graduated, he found that it was difficult—if not impossible—to find a job as a camera operator without actual work experience.

He was able to find a six-month unpaid internship at a community television station as a Production Assistant where he was able to get experience as a Camera Operator. Putting his internship experience on his résumé—along with letters of recommendation from producers and directors from the television station—greatly enhanced his chances of getting a paid position. At the community station, he was able to put together and edit a demo reel of television clips where he had served as a camera operator. His new résumé, letters of recommendation, and demo reel got him a job as a full-time camera operator at Turner Broadcasting Systems and a membership to the IATSE union.

Using an internship like Richard, Kim and others did could be just the edge you need to gain the experience and valuable professional contacts to land the job of your dreams.

You have digested more than half of this book, and I hope these secrets are making your mind explode with possibilities! Next, we're going to explore how volunteering can connect you to your next great job!

Chapter 5

Secret #5: Catapult Yourself into a New Field by Volunteering

I've heard people scoff at the prospect of volunteering because they don't want to work for free. I understand that, and I don't think you need to spend more than a few months at a job for which you're not paid—unless you want to.

You've already read about Marie, the Landscaper-turned-Ecologist, who volunteered on an environmental cleanup for less than a week and was immediately hired (because a key person noticed her) by the state of California.

The upside of volunteering is that it can directly lead to a job or can be used as experience on your résumé where you otherwise may have none. Many people walk out of a volunteering experience with *valuable contacts* in the industry and with excellent and influential *letters of recommendation*.

From Marine Lab Research Assistant to Dolphin Trainer

Name: Tim
Education: BS, Marine Biology
Current position: Marine Lab Research Assistant (salary not given)
Desired position: Dolphin Trainer (salary not given)

Let me tell you how Tim got to volunteer at a dream job that he was convinced would never be possible for him. Tim's story almost sounds like magic, but it's true. I first met Tim when he came to my private practice almost in a panic. It was 2005, and he had been laid off from his first job as a Research Assistant in a marine biology lab. Tim had earned his BS in Marine Biology the year before and took the first job he could find in his field as a researcher at a university lab.

He hated working indoors as a researcher. His vision was to get a job that was outdoors, hopefully on a field assignment out in the ocean. He believed it would be almost impossible to find such a coveted position without a Master's degree or a PhD.

I invited Tim to do an exercise that I had learned in the first book I'd ever read on career counseling: *Wishcraft* by Barbara Sher. The exercise is simple, but it can lead to miraculous results. I asked Tim to imagine that he had a life with no limitations. Factors like age, academic degree, geographic location, and prior experience didn't matter. I said, "If you had no limitations and could not fail, what would you do when you wake up tomorrow morning and could do any job you wanted?"

He couldn't picture the exact job, but he said he would like to have a job where he could look at the Pacific Ocean and that he would like to be living in Hawaii. Although he couldn't quite pinpoint the type of job that would make it possible, at least we were getting somewhere!

I wanted him to be more specific, and I had him write an exercise from my book, *Fearless Career Change called "Your Ideal Day".* For this exercise he was to go home and write a short story about one day in his life without limitations, including every detail of what he did from the moment he woke up in the morning to the moment he went to sleep. The story could be as fantastical as he wanted. There was only one stipulation—*the story had to include some sort of work* (a job) for which he was paid.

When he came back to my office a week later, he said that he was almost embarrassed to tell me the result of the exercise because it seemed too "impossible" and "unrealistic." His dream job was being a Dolphin Trainer!

I rarely, if ever, tell clients that their dream job (or something else that includes elements of the job they want) is impossible or a little bit "crazy."

He was shocked that I took him seriously, but I did. I quickly started thinking of solutions for his situation. I had seen two dolphin shows in my life. One was at SeaWorld in San Diego, and the other was at a Hilton hotel in Honolulu, Hawaii. Since his dream was to work in Hawaii, we started there.

My plan was that he would call whoever was in charge of the dolphin shows at the hotel and volunteer to act as an assistant. Sound far-fetched? I admit that it was a bit of a risk, but I got him to try it! It wasn't as difficult as it may sound.

I had Tim rehearse a ***phone script*** that I wrote for him, which summarized his education, work history, and desire to be a volunteer. It went something like this:

> "Hello, my name is Tim Wu. I have a BS in Marine Biology with ten months of work experience as a Research Assistant at a marine lab. I'm interested in becoming a Dolphin Trainer, and I'm looking for some hands-on experience and knowledge. I'd like to volunteer to work with you in any capacity as an assistant in your dolphin shows."

We wrote the thirty-second phone script on a piece of paper so he could read directly from the script and we rehearsed it a few times.

He called the main number for the hotel. A receptionist answered. Tim called and asked to be put through to the Dolphin Trainer. She said she didn't know how to reach her, but she offered to put him through to the special events department. Someone answered. He found out that the trainer was named Sandra and he got her direct phone number.

Tim called back, and with his eyes popping out of his head, he gave me a thumbs-up and repeated the phone script word-for-word.

Without even seeing Tim's résumé, Sandra said that she would be glad to have him as a volunteer!

What's your dream? What do you have to lose by trying to make it (or something similar) happen? Think as creatively and as proactively as you can—*even if you think it's impossible or if others tell you that it's impossible*!

Making Up for "No Experience"

Name: Shaniqua
Education: MS, Rehabilitation Counseling
Short-term goal: Volunteer
Long-term goal: Vocational Rehabilitation Counselor ($34,350 to $99,100)

Shaniqua had just graduated from a Master's program in Rehabilitation Counseling and wanted to work with a disabled population as a Vocational Rehabilitation Counselor. She had applied to jobs in private rehabilitation firms and in state and local government sectors, but she was not getting any interviews.

All of them demanded work experience, which she didn't have as a recent graduate. I advised her to try volunteering at a local nonprofit that helped veterans with service-related disabilities secure employment. She applied to a local nonprofit agency and got the volunteer opportunity.

She didn't get to perform actual counseling, but she did see clients and assist them with their résumés and interview coaching. She could use the experience on her résumé.

I strongly urged her to leverage her volunteer experience by getting a *letter of recommendation* from the Executive Director of the agency. She would be able to use it as "capital" to secure her next job.

She obtained the letter within four weeks of volunteering for the nonprofit. She loved the job and continued working there. After eight weeks, one of the nine rehabilitation staff members resigned.

The job opening was first announced internally (*not advertised*). She applied for the job and went through the interview process. She did well and was hired as a Rehabilitation Counselor.

Why would the agency spend the money and the time "ramping up" an outside employee when they had a high-performing volunteer candidate already working there who knew some of the policies, staff, and procedures of the agency?

Many companies—large and small—in private, public, and nonprofit sectors also have a policy of promoting from within. Some companies even offer bonuses to employees who can recommend a friend or colleague for an open position because it saves the company so much money without having to advertise a position and perform initial screening interviews. When you volunteer, you are a known entity, which is quite different from an unknown job applicant. The company has much less risk in hiring you than they would if you were a stranger applying to an Internet advertisement.

Doctorate in Medical Anthropology

Karla had a PhD in Medical Anthropology and her dissertation concerned the study of children's nutrition in indigenous societies. Although she enjoyed the theoretical side of earning her doctorate, she was much more committed to how she could pragmatically apply her knowledge to help children's hunger issues around the world. Her dream was to work as a consultant for The Hunger Project in New York. She got her start by volunteering for the Move for Hunger program in Asbury Park, New Jersey. With this experience, she was able to leverage a job as a Project Manager for The Hunger Project.

Use Volunteering on Your Résumé

Although volunteering is not paid, many employers view it as work experience. After all, she was given responsibilities and deadlines, was expected to arrive on time and report to a supervisor.

Whether your volunteer experience is just a way to put some work history on your résumé or a chance to get selected as a regular employee from within, it may be worthwhile to consider this strategy!

Chapter 6

Secret #6: Ascend the Ladder from an Entry-Level Position to an Executive Position

From Administrative Assistant to Director of Operations

Name: Darlene
Education: BA, Sociology
Present job: Administrative Assistant ($21,460 to $56,960)
Target job: Director of Operations ($49,240 to $187,200 or more)

Darlene, a receptionist in a dental office with a BA in Sociology, had a can-do attitude. She had exceptional customer service skills and an impeccable work ethic along with expert-level skills in Microsoft Word, Excel, PowerPoint, Access, Outlook, and Publisher. (You can also receive free self-paced *advanced certificates* in these Microsoft Office programs in the self-paced online programs at www.gcflearnfree.org.)

She had her eye on an Administrative Assistant position and wanted to climb the corporate ladder in the Fortune 100 sector. She found an entry-level job at Oracle, which was number eighty in the Fortune 100 sector at the time. She broke in as an Administrative Assistant to a Manager in the operations department. Soon, she gained the admiration and trust of her boss.

Learning on Her Own

She got permission from her boss to take an in-house sponsored training in project management that was teaching Agile/Scrum methodologies. She learned Microsoft Project and obtained a Six Sigma Black Belt at no cost, in twelve weeks, at a local One-Stop Career Center. After earning these project-management and quality-control skills, she was given increasing responsibilities. When her boss was promoted, she was able to assume her boss's position as an Operations Manager. Two years later, she was promoted from within to an Operations Director, traveling the world and making more than $200,000 a year.

From Network Administrator to IT Senior Manager

Name: Carlos
Present job: Network Administrator ($48,260 to $121,090)
Target job: Senior IT Manager ($87,910 to $187,200 or more)

Carlos broke in to an entry-level position with a vocational certificate as a CCNA (Cisco-Certified Network Administrator) specializing in VOIP (Voice-Operated Internet Protocols) at AT&T. At the time, the world's largest telecommunications company was number twenty-two on the Fortune 100 list.

After a time, he was promoted to a Network Engineer and he gained an appreciation of network security. He decided to study Cybersecurity on his own at www.lynda.com to upgrade his skills. After three years, while gaining even more knowledge of the field of network security on the job, he was promoted to a senior management position, earning more than $180,000 a year.

From Television Production Assistant to Executive in Charge of Production

Name: Martin
Present job: Film Production Assistant – nonunion - (about $350 per day)
Target job: Executive in Charge of Production (about $8,000 per month)

Martin had an MFA (Master of Fine Arts) with an emphasis in film. He had made his own student films and wanted to break into the film industry as a screenwriter/director. Some people are able to do this, but it is rare. If you want to be part of the coveted entertainment industry, you most likely will have to start at the bottom and work your way up—no matter what your university degree. Michael started as a Production Assistant by volunteering on a six-day shoot of a short film. The Script Supervisor on the film saw his hard work and recommended that he be hired on another (nonunion) position as a Production Assistant on a feature-length film. On his next film, he was promoted to Assistant Director. After years of learning on the set, working on various projects, and learning behind the scenes, he got the chance to be a Supervising Producer (Executive in Charge of Production) on a television show. Only at that point, six years later, did he get the opportunity and meet the right contacts to direct a film of his own.

Front Desk to General Manager of a Hotel

Name: Jared
Education: AA, Hospitality
Short-Term Goal: Hotel Front Desk Clerk ($19,320 to $34,990)
Long-Term Goal: Hotel General Manager ($49,240 to $187,200 or more)

Jared loved the field of hotels, travel, and event planning. His goal was to become a General Manager at a large hotel. He majored in Hospitality and knew he would have to start from the bottom if he were to advance to an executive level. He spent six months at a front desk job at a Marriott hotel and was quickly promoted to Front Desk Manager.

After two years, he realized that it would be good for him to learn as many job functions as possible to understand the workings of the hotel. He took an Ed2Go class in Event Planning and advanced to the Catering Manager in charge of special events. After doing quite well in that job and helping to host conferences with more than a thousand attendees, he decided to take an online class in Hospitality Management for less than

$200 from www.study.com. This prepared him to move up to Assistant General Manager and finally to his long-term goal of General Manager.

From Entry to Entrepreneur

Another way to get to the top is, of course, being your own boss. Can you see yourself as the president, owner, or CEO of your own business?

Name: Latisha
Education: BS, Computer Sciences
Short-term goal: Web Developer in a large company ($34,320 to $112,160)
Long-term goal: Owner of a web-development company (She started at less than she made at the large company, but her income became almost unlimited as she built her company—and she enjoyed being her own boss.)

Latisha had her Bachelor's degree in Computer Sciences, specializing in Web Development, and she easily worked her way into a Fortune 1000 company as a Web Designer.

When she tried to determine whether she wanted to start her own business, I recommended that she go to www.sba.gov (U.S. Small Business Administration) and find a government-based Small Business Development Center near her home in Seattle.

She was able to find a business mentor who could meet with her free of charge at *www.score.org*. At the Small Business Development Center, she took several courses in:

- writing a business plan
- accounting and bookkeeping for small businesses
- marketing
- forming a business entity
- funding for small businesses

All the courses were *free*. In addition, her mentor helped her fill out all of the papers she needed to secure a loan to start her business. When she first began she could not afford a full-time office space. She was able to rent executive office space by the hour from www.regus.com to meet with important clients in a professional setting. She also got a free listing in the Internet Yellow Pages (www.yp.com), which put her business on the first page of the results for a Google search of Web Designers in her area. She got her own website and slowly built a successful business through her website, Internet "ad word" advertising and word of mouth.

If you're willing to start with an entry-level position and take advantage of on-the-job training or obtain training on your own while on the job, you may have what it takes to be promoted to a higher position. Even if you don't know everything about your new position, you have the type of personality and confidence it takes to *learn while doing*.

You also might consider becoming an entrepreneur. If you do decide to start your own business, be sure to take advantage of some or all of the free and extremely low-cost options listed above!

Chapter 7

Secret #7: Gain Work Experience in a Part-Time, Flexible Job with Benefits

Most employers would rather bet on a student or graduate with *some* kind of real-world work experience (***even if unrelated to their major*** or their long-term goals) than a candidate with no work experience at all.

Working helps students and grads with work experience. It helps instill:

- work ethic
- knowledge of business practices
- interpersonal communication
- understanding of company or corporate culture
- responsibility
- competence
- sensitivity to diversity
- teamwork
- transferable and job-related skills
- ability to follow directions
- practice in completing assigned tasks
- punctuality
- ability to meet deadlines *and more*

While it may seem ideal to finish your degree as quickly as possible while carrying a full class load and having free time to study, some sort of part-time work might make you ***more marketable*** in the long run. It can be:

- something you can list on your résumé
- a big boost for your job application
- a confidence builder
- a source for work references
- a great way to get letters of recommendation
- a source of stories about real-life accomplishments at an interview

If you'd like to build your work experience for the first time, consider finding a job with benefits and flexible, part-time hours that can give you the ability to plan your work around your classes.

Types of Benefits

While none of the following part-time jobs offer particularly high wages, they do carry benefits to part-time (and often flexibly scheduled) workers. All of the companies listed below offer some combination of benefits and perks like medical, dental, vision, and life insurance.

They also may offer paid sick, vacation, and holidays off. Some offer 401(k), retirement, stock options, employee discounts, domestic partner and family health care, tuition reimbursement, profit sharing, elder care and child care.

Most have a minimum number of hours you must work per week to qualify for benefits—fifteen to thirty hours is common. Most also have a minimum time you must have worked there, such as an average of ninety days to qualify, but a few of them ***start benefits in the first week of work***!

Large National Companies That Offer Part-Time Jobs with Benefits

I suggest that you research these opportunities carefully to determine how many hours you can work and what kind of benefits you'd like. These well-known companies offer ***part-time work with benefits***, but many smaller, lesser-known companies offer similar options.

- Costco
- Lowe's
- Lands' End
- Barnes and Noble
- UPS
- JPMorgan Chase
- Staples
- Trader Joe's
- REI
- Home Depot
- Nike
- Starbucks
- U-Haul
- Wegman's
- Whole Foods
- Safeway

Many banks, credit unions, hospitals, retail outlets, department stores, and grocery stores also offer part-time options with benefits.

In fact, what a ***great deal*** this is! UPS offers health and other benefits that kick in after only thirty days of employment and a fifteen-hour workweek! I suggest that you visit the websites of these companies or go to a physical location to find out more about part-time work with benefits!

Another way to find part-time jobs is to go to a job search engine like monster.com or indeed.com and type "part-time" in the search box next to the position you desire plus the city in which you're looking. For example, "part-time Customer Service Representative, Las Vegas, NV."

As we come to the conclusion of this book, you have seven exciting secrets you can use to get from studies to success!

Let's take a look at one more thing: your magnificent brain!

Conclusion

Your Magnificent Brain

A s you move forward in life, don't underestimate the wondrous power of your brain!

While you are sleeping, your brain creates **thousands** of new brain cells. When you wake up, you can **program** or assign these brand-new neurons to either negative (pessimistic) neuro-pathways or positive (optimistic) ones. You can say, "Oh, I have to face another awful day" or "Wow—another **great** day of surprises." Both send very different messages to your brain. While this may be obvious, these modes of thinking can be scientifically measured down to the cellular level with biochemistry, biophysics, and neuropsychology.

Epigenetics

Your mind and your thoughts form microscopic strands of cells in your physical brain. The more strands that are built along **positive** neural pathways, the more proteins your genes (DNA) will express in **positive attitudes**, good health, happiness, and productive actions. This new science, the core of which neuropsychologists call *neuroplasticity*, is sometimes referred to as *epigenetics*.

The New Psychology

At first, your thoughts may seem automatic or habitual, but modern cognitive behavioral and positive psychology and the metaphysical field of intention and manifestation tells us we are largely responsible for choosing our own thoughts. Choose to decide you are fully capable of finding and doing your dream job and getting well paid to do it rather than saying, "I will never be able to do what I want to do—there is just too much competition out there."

Some fascinating books delve much more deeply into the workings of the brain, thinking, emotions and beliefs:

- *Switch on Your Brain* by Dr. Caroline Leaf
- *The Biology of Belief* by Dr. Bruce Lipton
- *The Genie in Your Genes* by Dr. Dawson Church
- *Molecules of Emotion* by Dr. Candace B. Pert

Two Secrets to Successful Thinking and Planning

Two capabilities of your brain are key secrets to your success (which are borne out in scientific evidence):

1. Setting goals
2. Guided visualization

One of the wealthiest steel magnates of the industrial age, Andrew Carnegie, wrote this goal for himself:

> I demand riches in definite terms. I have a definite plan for acquiring riches. I am engaged in carrying out my plan, and I give the equivalent in useful services of the riches that I demand.

You have the ***power to choose*** the "riches" you demand (salary, health, and happiness) and the "useful services" (work, career, effort, and time) that you exchange for those riches!

Writing Your Goals

I'd like you to take note of a study by psychologist Dr. Gail Matthews of Dominican University. The study shows that **writing** down your goals (rather than not having goals or just keeping them in your head), sharing your goals with someone else (such as an *accountability partner*), and reporting your progress to your partner once a week makes you significantly more likely to attain your goals.

The Reticular-Activating System

Many peak performance coaches, writers, and speakers like Brian Tracy (*Create Your Own Future*), Tony Robbins (*Awaken the Giant Within*), Bob Proctor (*You Were Born Rich*) and others attribute the efficacy of setting goals to a part of the brain called the *reticular activating system* (RAS).

The RAS is located in the base of the brain, and it can selectively filter, focus and pay attention to whatever we deem to be important to us. By **telling your brain** that earning a certain amount of money or achieving a certain measure of health or a certain type of job is important to you, the RAS actually helps us attend to **cues** in the environment to those stimuli that **lead** us to our most important goals.

Since the brain's central purpose is to ensure our survival, if we choose goals that will **enhance** our survival, the RAS will help us selectively focus on thinking and behaving in a way that will accomplish those goals. You can set and write down goals for your grades, your career, your finances, and even your relationships.

This is your life! It's worth it to think carefully about what you want and implement written plans to achieve it. You can do it!

Guided Visualization

What do female and male Olympic athletes, the San Francisco 49ers, Tiger Woods, Oprah Winfrey, Jim Carrey, Arnold Schwarzenegger, and Will Smith have in common besides being famous? They all use *visualization* to achieve their goals.

Visualization, simply put, means creating a picture or movie (sometimes with sounds, smells, emotions, and other sensory information) in your own mind of yourself in an imaginary scene doing, getting, or experiencing something you would like to achieve *as if it were occurring now* or in the future.

If a coach or a therapist is guiding you through the experience, it is called *guided visualization*. Visualization is somewhat like meditation; it is usually done with your eyes closed and your muscles relaxed.

- Tiger Woods pictures a perfect golf swing with the ball dropping right into the cup and his elation that he has won the game *before* he takes the actual swing

- A quarterback conjures up a feeling of deep satisfaction and excitement as he completes the perfect touchdown pass *before* he steps up to the playing field

- An entertainer sees and hears the audience clapping and cheering while feeling unbelievably proud of her exceptional performance *before* the curtain opens and she steps onto the stage

- *You* picture yourself in the job of your dreams, *imagine* hearing the voices of a supportive boss and friendly coworkers complimenting you on the good work you're doing. You actually *feel* the satisfaction of seeing your bank account growing!

I have been using guided visualization for over 20 years with my classes and clients. I use it often help them picture their perfect day at their perfect job or feeling relaxed and absolutely confident at an interview that ends with a generous job offer.

Does this sound unbelievable or like a bunch of hocus-pocus?

Dr. Lynn Joseph

Let's look at some evidence that guided visualization really works. Clinical psychologist Dr. Lynn Joseph studied people who had recently been laid off. She split her subjects into two groups.

- Participants in the guided visualization group listened (six times over two weeks) to a twenty-minute recording of a script that guided them through their last day of work at their last job and into the future. Participants were able to "complete" and "release" negative feelings about their last jobs. Then, they visualized themselves in the future receiving the job offer of their choice.

- Participants in the other group simply visualized themselves (six times over two weeks) doing job-search related activities.

Results indicated that at four-month follow-ups, rates of full-time reemployment were significantly higher for the first group of visualization participants than for the second. Of the participants in the *first group* who resolved emotions about the past and pictured an ideal job offer in the future, *72 percent* were reemployed within four months. For the *second group*, only *39 percent* found employment in the same time period.

Dr. Joseph's pioneering study (www.joblossrecovery.com) was independently assessed and recognized by SAMHSA, US Department of Health and Human Services. Her study was published in the peer-reviewed *Journal of Consulting Psychology*.

Dr. Emmett Miller

Another expert in guided visualization and noted pioneer of the mind/body medicine movement is Dr. Emmett Miller. You may enjoy his inspiring and effective guided visualizations on peak performance and success (www.drmiller.com).

His CDs and MP3 downloads for "Awakening the Leader Within"

and "I Can: Achieving Self-Empowerment" are terrific ways to program yourself for peak performance in personal and professional endeavors.

My Wish for You

You are a ***unique and magnificently created*** human being. No one else in the world was put here—by genetic, natural, or divine purpose—to do what you are meant to do.

I encourage you to believe in yourself and love yourself wherever you are in your education, career, earning potential, or life's path. You are the key to your own progress and potential.

I hope that these seven secrets along with setting enticing but attainable goals and visualizing them as if they have already been achieved catapults you to a new confidence and fulfillment of your career dreams and life purpose!

Marky is available for college and corporate speaking engagements/ radio/television/webinars on a number of career-development, job-seeking, personal/professional goals, and motivational/inspirational messages. She can be reached on www.linkedin.com/in/markystein or marky@markystein.com.

She has done presentations for the following colleges and universities:

- Benedictine University, Chicago, Illinois
- California Baptist University, Riverside, California
- City of Seattle University, Seattle, Washington
- Elon University, Elon, Pennsylvania
- Fairleigh Dickenson University, Florham, New Jersey
- Florida International University Alumni Association, Miami, Florida
- Georgia State University, Atlanta, Georgia
- Knox College, Galesburg, Illinois
- Millersville University, Millersville, Pennsylvania
- North Carolina State University, Raleigh, North Carolina
- North Dakota State University, Fargo, North Dakota
- Rochester Institute of Technology, Rochester, New York
- San Jose City Evergreen College District, San Jose, California
- Stanford University Career Center, Stanford, California
- State University of New York at Albany, Albany, New York
- State University of New York, Empire College, Saratoga Springs, New York
- Stony Brook University, Stony Brook, New York
- Texas Christian University, Fort Worth, Texas
- Tufts University, Medford, Massachusetts
- University of California at Riverside, Riverside, California
- University of Colorado Springs, Colorado Springs, Colorado
- University of Florida, Gainesville, Florida
- University of Hawaii, Hilo, Hawaii
- University of Iowa Alumni Association, Iowa City, Iowa
- University of Miami, Miami, Florida

- University of Missouri, Saint Louis, Missouri
- University of Rochester Alumni Exchange, Rochester, New York
- University of South Carolina, Columbia, South Carolina
- West Valley College Faculty, Saratoga, California
- Western New England University, Springfield, Massachusetts
- Western Washington University, Bellingham, Washington

Marky is also available for one-on-one career coaching at marky@markystein.com

If you are interested in becoming a Certified Career Coach, contact Marky's Institute for Career Coaching and Development at www.instituteccd.com.

Index

A

accredited certificates xviii, 38
adjunct professor 37
administrative assistant 12, 38, 59
agile/Scrum 36, 38, 60
American Job Centers xviii, 32
Anthony Robbins ix
anthropology xiii, 8, 58
anxiety xvii
approach letter 50
art xiii, xiv, 5, 27, 33, 34, 38, 51
art director 33, 34
associates 2, 33, 41, 45
attorney 23, 41, 44
AutoCAD 38, 51, 52

B

bachelor's xi, xii, xiii, xv, 2, 5, 8, 31,
        33, 36, 41, 45, 46, 48, 49, 62
Barbara Sher i, ix, 55, 79
biochemistry xiii, 2, 34, 67
biology xiii, xvi, 2, 3, 4, 41, 54, 55,
        56, 68
brain 66, 67, 68, 69
branding xviii, 40

B

business administration xiii, 7, 35,
        36, 62

C

career change i, xi, xv, xvii, xviii,
        40, 55
career counselor 6, 10, 43
career-interest assessment 6
certificate xv, xviii, 2, 3, 6, 7, 8, 10,
        16, 21, 22, 29, 30, 32, 33, 34,
        35, 36, 38, 40, 44, 45, 59, 60
chemist 35
chemistry xiii, xv, 35, 41
classic literature xiii, 9
cold calls 4
college recruiter 48, 50
competition i, xviii, 47, 49, 68
computer information systems
        xiii, 36
computer sciences xiii, 36, 46, 49, 62
computer-user support
        technician 36
conservation scientist 41
continuing education units 29
copyeditor 9, 13
copywriter 5

creative writing xiii, 5
customer service 3, 4, 35, 36, 37, 59, 66

D

depression xvii
direct contact techniques 49
director of operations 59
dolphin trainer xvi, 54, 55, 56
Dr. Bruce Lipton 68
Dr. Candace B. Pert 68
Dr. Caroline Leaf 68
Dr. Dawson Church 68
dream job xi, xv, xviii, 9, 55, 68
Dr. Emmett Miller 71
Dr. Lynn Joseph 71

E

ecologist xv, 41, 54
Ed2Go 3, 6, 7, 8, 9, 10, 61
editor 6, 9, 13, 28
educational counseling (career counseling) xiii, 43, 55
electrical engineering xiii, 41, 48
entrepreneur 25, 62, 63
entry-level xiv, xvi, 10, 21, 31, 33, 36, 48, 59, 60, 63
environmental studies xiii, 42
event planner 10, 24, 45
executive in charge of production xvi, 60, 61

F

Fearless Career Change i, xi, 55
film xiii, 51, 60, 61
film assistant director 51
film production assistant 60
Fortune 100 iii, xi, xiv, 48, 59, 60, 79

Fortune 500 iii, xii, xiv, xv, xvi, xvii, xviii, 10, 31, 35, 38, 44, 45, 46, 47, 62, 79
Fortune 1000 xiv, 10, 47, 48, 49, 50, 52
frustration xvii

G

gerontology 8, 22
grant writer 5, 8
graphic artist 34

H

high school diploma xiii, 2, 4
home-based business 7, 25
hospitality xiii, 61
hotel front desk clerk 61
hotel general manager 61
human resources xiii, 15, 39, 43, 44, 45, 49, 50
human resources manager 44, 50

I

intern 10, 47, 48, 49, 51, 52
IT senior manager 60

L

lab technician xv, 35
landscaper 41, 54
law xiii, xv, 22, 23, 44
lawyer 33, 34, 44
liberal studies xiii, 45
life coaching 30
logistics xiii, 12, 34, 35, 51
logistics technician 34, 35
long-term goal xiv, xix, 2, 6, 8, 10, 29, 30, 33, 34, 35, 49, 51, 52, 57, 61, 62, 64

M

major xi, xvi, xvii, xix, 9, 20, 30, 34, 35, 41, 42, 61, 64
marine biology xiii, xvi, 54, 55, 56
marine lab research assistant 54
marketability xviii, 32, 33
marketing xiii, 6, 7, 10, 20, 24, 30, 31, 37, 38, 39, 40, 41, 45, 62
marketing and communications manager 10
marketing manager 30
marketing research analyst 37, 38
marketing specialist 30
master's xi, xii, xv, 2, 3, 8, 33, 35, 41, 42, 43, 44, 48, 51, 55, 57
mechanical drafter 34, 51, 52
mechanical engineer 51, 52
mechanical engineering xiv, 51, 52
medical anthropology 58
medical billing and coding 7, 22
mentor 62, 63
Myers-Briggs Type Indicator 9

N

network administrator 34, 38, 60
no experience 57
nonprofit xv, 6, 8, 20, 37, 50, 57, 58
nursing xiv, 7
nutrition 21, 30, 58

O

One-Stop Career Centers 32, 33, 35, 38, 52, 60
O*NET 1, 2, 6
O*NET Interest Profiler 6
online self-paced classes xviii
Open University 42, 43, 44

P

paid internship 51
paralegal xv, 22, 23, 34
part-time job xix, 65, 66
personality preference test 9
pharmacist 33, 34
pharmacy xiv, 21, 34
pharmacy technician 21, 34
PhD ii, xiii, 9, 29, 37, 55, 58
phone script 56
physical therapist 2, 3, 5
physical therapist aide 2, 3
physical therapy xiv, xv, 2, 3, 4, 5, 6, 21
political science xiv, 34
professional association 45
program manager 44, 48
project manager 14, 16, 35, 36, 37, 39, 58
promotion xviii, 44
psychology xiv, 29, 30, 43, 68, 71
public administration xiv, 44
public health xiv, 44
public health administrator 44
public health educator 44
Python 26, 36

R

radio and television broadcasting xiv, 52
raise xii, xviii, 40, 44, 46
rebranding 30, 45
registered nurse 7
résumé ii, xviii, xix, 3, 4, 5, 8, 30, 36, 38, 40, 41, 42, 43, 44, 45, 46, 47, 48, 52, 54, 56, 57, 58, 65

S

salary xv, xix, 1, 2, 5, 6, 8, 33, 35, 36,
        44, 48, 51, 54, 68
salary information 1, 2
Salesforce 31, 35
Salesforce developer 35
short-term goal 2, 6, 8, 10, 29, 30, 33,
        34, 35, 49, 51, 52, 57, 61, 62
Six Sigma Black Belt 39, 60
skills xi, xii, xviii, xix, 1, 5, 8, 11, 12,
        13, 14, 15, 17, 18, 19, 20, 21, 22,
        23, 24, 26, 27, 28, 30, 33, 36,
        37, 38, 43, 48, 52, 59, 60, 64
social work xiv, 8
social worker 8
sociology xiv, 37, 59
software engineer xv, 35, 36, 45,
        49, 51
software engineering xiv, 35, 51
stage manager 51
start-up xvii
stipend 47, 48, 51
supply chain manager 34, 35

T

target job xvii, 5, 7, 9, 35, 36, 37, 41,
        43, 44, 45, 59, 60
technical recruiter 43
technical writer 5, 6
television camera operator 52
television production assistant xvi,
        52, 60
theater arts xiv, 51
transferrable skills 37

U

unpaid internship 47, 52

V

veterinarian 6, 7, 21
veterinary assistant 6, 7, 21
veterinary medicine xiv, 6
vocational rehabilitation
        counseling xiv
vocational rehabilitation counselor
        xv, 57
volunteering xiv, xviii, 10, 42, 43, 53,
        54, 57, 58, 61

W

web developer 39, 62
wellness coach 29, 30
work experience xix, 52, 56, 57, 58,
        64, 65
writing tutor 9
www.barbarasher.com i
www.coursera.com 29
www.data.com 8, 50
www.DrLynnJoseph.com ii
www.drmiller.com 71
www.ed2go.com 3
www.edx.com 29
www.gcflearnfree.org 29, 59
www.humanmetrics.com 9
www.indeed.com 49
www.onetonline.org 1
www.sba.gov 7, 62
www.score.org 7, 62
www.servicelocator.org 32, 39
www.study.com 29, 62
www.universalclass.com 29

Z

zoology xiv, 6

About the Author

 Marky Stein is a three-time best-selling author of the renowned "Fearless" career series, a Fortune 100 consultant, a contributor to the *Wall Street Journal*, a career coach, and a college and corporate speaker. Ms. Stein's *Fearless Interviewing* was hailed as one of the "100 Best Career Books of All Time" by onlinecollege. org and is ranked number two of the "100 Inspirational Books Every Job Seeker Should Read" by onlineuniversities.com.

Barbara Sher, PBS television personality, life coach, and *New York Times* best-selling author of *Wishcraft*, calls Marky's books "clear, kind, wise, practical, inspired, and full of good advice."

From Freshman to Fortune 500: Seven Secrets to Success for Grads, Undergrads, and Career Changers is based on her more than twenty years of actual career-counseling experience, coaching students and executives in just about every industry and walk of life.

The author was recently named by the popular networking site, LinkedIn, as "one of the nation's top career experts." She is also on the Advisory Board of College Recruiter, rated by Forbes as one of the leading job search websites for internships and entry level positions in the world. She resides in a beach house in Santa Cruz, California, where she writes, meditates, hikes, trains other career coaches, and enjoys the sunshine.

www.ingramcontent.com/pod-product-compliance
Lightning Source LLC
Chambersburg PA
CBHW030907180526
45163CB00004B/1740